MANAGING CHANGE FOR LIBRARY SUPPORT STAFF

Managing Change for Library Support Staff

ANNE GOULDING
Department of Information and Library Studies
Loughborough University

Avebury

Aldershot • Brookfield USA • Hong Kong • Singapore • Sydney

Published by
Avebury
Ashgate Publishing Limited
Gower House
Croft Road
Aldershot
Hants GU11 3HR
England

Ashgate Publishing Company
Old Post Road
Brookfield
Vermont 05036
USA

British Library Cataloguing in Publication Data

Goulding, Anne
    Managing change for library support staff
    1. Libraries – Management   2. Library administration   3. Library
    employees   4. Library personnel management   5. Organizational
    change
    I. Title
    025.1

    ISBN 1 85972 249 0

Library of Congress Catalog Card Number: 96-83216

Printed and bound by Athenaeum Press, Ltd.,
Gateshead, Tyne & Wear.

Contents

List of tables

Acknowledgements

Many thanks to all the staff in the case study authorities who gave so freely of their time and opinions. Their friendliness, interest and openness ensured that the field work for this book was both stimulating and enjoyable. I am particularly indebted to Bob Usherwood for his constant support and intellectual contributions during my time as a PhD student. Thanks also to Carolyn Pritchett for her careful proof-reading. Finally, thanks to all my colleagues, friends and family for their encouragement.

Introduction

> A manager can look upon ... change as a doomsday crisis or as a
> challenge in which the major concern is to maintain both quality
> of product and commitment to the human resources of the
> organization (Lippet and Lippet, 1984, p. 15).

It is part of the manager's job to develop the organization by introducing
steady, predictable change. The pressures in today's environment, however,
mean that change is often irregular, unplanned and erratic. This book is an
attempt to describe how external environmental and internal organizational
changes have affected the staff of library services, focusing specifically on
support staff who, being at the sharp end of the service, have to cope with
the effects of change on a daily basis. The book is also concerned with
identifying strategies that managers can use to regulate the effects of change
on their support staff and so ensure a productive working environment.

This introduction reviews some of the more important changes that
libraries have experienced and are currently experiencing. Economic,
political, and social changes have all had an effect on library services and
have resulted in new structures, new services and new ways of working.
Those at operational, as opposed to managerial level, are charged with
translating these policy changes into practice and, therefore, are particularly
exposed to the effects of reorganization and change. How management
responds in these circumstances is also crucial in ensuring that staff are able
to cope and adapt to new pressures and demands. Thus, the staff
management issues arising out of this changing climate are outlined in this
chapter.

The changing climate

Libraries, like other organizations, are dependent on the fortunes of their parent institution and external events. Changes in the organization's policies and prosperity, user preferences and needs, increases in costs and decreases in funds all make it essential for library managers to gain a thorough understanding of the environment they are operating within and to sharpen their organization's responsiveness to external change (Moran, 1980).

Significant external pressures have had a considerable impact on libraries and their staff, and have forced library managers to question much they once took for granted. It is possible to construct a long list of changes taking place in the current library environment, e.g. the 'information explosion' and new forms of technology and media to handle it, electronic publishing, changes in how libraries are financed, quality measures, performance assessment and indicators. All mean that library managers must stay alert to environmental developments and how those developments are likely to affect their own services.

There are signs that policy makers are becoming increasingly aware of the magnitude of changes facing libraries, with the result that a number of important pieces of research and subsequent reports have recently been commissioned. The Follet (Joint Funding Councils' Libraries Review Group, 1993) and Fielden (John Fielden Consultancy, 1993) reports were a result of concern on the part of the higher education funding councils that a number of developments, i.e. the growth of student numbers, changes in teaching technologies, and economic factors, were causing problems in libraries (House, and Moon, 1994). Similarly, Aslib's public library review (Aslib, 1995) had the task of investigating the public library's environment, users' and non-users' opinions, attitudes and behaviours, and the public library's functions and services in an environment of great social, technological, demographic and economic change. A new Library and Information Commission and a new Advisory Council on public libraries have also recently been established with the aims of taking library services forward and finding ways of coping with the multitude of changes taking place.

Technological, socio-political, human and demographic factors all affect library and information units directly or indirectly, but it is economic factors that are most significant because change in the economic environment is usually effected the most quickly (Martyn, 1991).

Economic change

Financial support for libraries relies upon the party in power's economic ideology, priorities and budgetary balance and, for the last fifteen years or so,

2

general economic problems have led to a severe erosion of library budgets. The effects of this austerity have been experienced across the whole spectrum of library and information services. The outcome is a cheerless situation in which the organization has to sacrifice certain desirable or essential conditions often resulting in a lack of progression and even regression (Harvey and Spyers-Duran, 1984).

In the public library sector, decreasing grants from central to local government have led to cuts in local authority services across the board with libraries often suffering disproportionately (Martyn, 1991). This has been accompanied by pressure upon public libraries to raise income from both local and central government for practical and philosophical reasons.

The emphasis on reducing public expenditure, value for money and self sufficiency have encouraged all library services to increase productivity and efficiency including those in the academic library sector. The Annual Library Statistics from the Library and Information Statistics Unit (Sumsion et al, 1995) show that in the old universities library expenditure represented 2.87 per cent of the total university recurrent expenditure in 1993/4 compared with 3.26 per cent in 1983/4, and this was while student numbers continued to grow. These changes have been accompanied by a new budgetary regime with the devolution of financial controls to cost centres and the predominance of the concept of the budget centre. To show how in tune they are with the enterprise culture and to make up for cuts in universities' grants, academic libraries, too, have gone down the road of income generation. According to one estimate, academic libraries earn about 10% of their total income from charges of one sort or another (Winkworth, 1994).

Most special libraries have also undergone major upheavals and restructuring in an age of substantial organizational change during which special librarians have been asked to perform amazing feats of budgetary cuts and have been subject to a constant succession of absolute cuts. These have resulted in lean and efficient departments as year on year expenditure reductions of 50% have not been uncommon (Cropley, 1992). Special librarians are generally now asked to justify their own existence in a written report listing the purposes of the library and the consequences of eliminating it (Daum, 1987).

The impact of wider economic trends can be observed in many areas of working life in libraries and not all need have had a completely detrimental effect. However, relationships, career opportunities, motivation and morale have probably all been affected in some way. The economic health of the nation will have repercussions on the lives of individual workers too. Inflation rates, interest rates and house prices are just a few of the factors which will affect people in their day-to-day lives and may well have

3

consequences in the workplace. Job mobility and security, for example, could become important issues for the individual living within a volatile economy.

Administrative changes

Public libraries have been going through a period of bureaucratic change since local government reorganization in 1974. Many public library departments have since been absorbed into larger directorates such as Leisure or Education with a subsequent effect on patterns of service provision (McKee, 1987). This emergence of corporate management in local authorities and the absorption of many library services into larger directorates have demanded a change of outlook on behalf of the staff operating those services. These moves have been reflected at national level with the establishment of the Department of National Heritage replacing the old Office of Arts and Libraries.

The current proposals to restructure local government again in favour of unitary authorities in England and Wales will have far reaching repercussions for public library services and their staff. The Library Association fears that:

> ...where a move to a unitary authority involves the dismantling
> and dispersal of an existing public library service, the result will
> be disruption in the short term, no guarantee of improved service
> in the long term and an inevitable increase in costs (Assistant
> Librarian, 1991, p. 114).

Similarly the higher education sector has experienced a period of rapid change following the merger of the university and polytechnic sectors. 'Convergence' in higher education, i.e. the merging of the library and information/computing services, is also causing substantial restructuring. The Fielden Report (John Fielden Consultancy, 1993) distinguishes between organizational and operational convergence. The former rarely causes changes to operational practices while the latter can effect major upheaval as the information and library services come together in day-to-day operations.

For the commercial and private sectors the 1980s was a decade of intensive merger and acquisition activity. This facilitated significant changes in the user groups of special libraries. It also often meant an alteration to reporting relationships and the division within which the library or information units was located (Cropley, 1992).

4

Changing political priorities and social attitudes

Certain principles of national government policy have particular relevance for the future of library services. The commitment to reduce public spending; the encouragement and incentives given to private sector firms to move into public service provision; the attempt to redefine the functions of government and make everything subject to market forces, culminating in the charter movement, have all contributed to a changing climate in which adaptation, reorientation and responsiveness are essential.

The determination to reduce public expenditure is thus not just a response to economic difficulties but an article of faith which demands that the private sector should be encouraged at the expense of the public sector. King (1989) asserts that, in the 1980s,

> What was once considered economic necessity became an ideological weapon under the leadership of Mrs Thatcher. Committed to a policy of self-reliance, the government absorbed the cuts in public expenditure into a political philosophy which expounded the necessity of reducing state intervention in all its forms (p. 39).

Today, the market judges everything and information is now seen as a commodity, not a service to be given away at public expense, "in terms of measurable activity rather than as a generalised public good" (Henty, 1989, p. 177). Libraries today are feeling the same kinds of effectiveness pressures that most organizations are experiencing as they are expected to do more with less (Maehr, 1989). Every item of expenditure is now rigorously scrutinised and libraries are among the most vulnerable departments because of their large operating costs and low, or no, profits (Ungarelli and McNierney, 1983).

For public libraries, the introduction of compulsory tendering for some local services has led to the scrutiny of the performance of all (Coleman, 1990). Despite the fears of many in the public library sector, compulsory competitive tendering has not been extended to public library services. The KPMG Peat Marwick (1994) study of the pilot projects set up by the Department of National Heritage reported very strong feelings against compulsory contracting out and found that some services are much more conducive to contracting out than others. The report concluded that there is some market interest in library services but it will be some time before contracting out becomes more widespread. The main point that seems to emerge from the study is the increasingly common use of the ideology of market place in public libraries.

In academic libraries too, the charter movement has turned students into consumers and, as a result, increased their awareness of their rights as "fully paid-up members of a university" (House and Moon, 1994, p. 75). Increasing pressure for accountability, value for money, quality, and efficiency raises important questions about structures and the management of staff.

Reorganization of staffing structures

The Fielden Report (John Fielden Consultancy, 1993) summarises the important changes taking place in academic library staffing structures and responsibilities and draws attention to the expansion of the paraprofessional role. Economic pressures, support staff career development issues, and technology have all resulted in a shift in job responsibilities in academic libraries. In fact, technology has been an extremely important catalyst for change as far as staffing structures are concerned. Fielden reports how technology is likely to facilitate future changes in the duties, roles and responsibilities of staff. Similarly, in public libraries the automation of many routine operations is changing how work is planned and approached (Cowan and Usherwood, 1992).

The Fielden Report (John Fielden Consultancy, 1993) describes how, as professional librarians concentrate on learner support, paraprofessionals are increasingly taking over cataloguing, and even classification with the support of automated systems. Support staff are also increasingly responsible for enquiry desks and handle the bulk of queries leaving only a few subject-based questions for the information specialist to answer. Fielden also predicts that the number of paraprofessional staff will grow and will continue to take over tasks hitherto performed by professionals as those professional librarians concentrate more on working with their academic colleagues in a wide range of support activities. The work formerly undertaken by these professionals is thus increasingly performed by assistants as the professionals need to free themselves of as many routine operations as possible. In these circumstances the library assistant's role is becoming 'up-skilled'.

Similar developments have been occurring in public libraries for many years. As public spending declines and, consequently, public library budgets contract, management will be eager to employ more cost effective workforce strategies (Levett, 1981). Oulton (1991) maintains that revisions to public library staffing establishments may have occurred anyway without the pressure for financial savings, but an immediate objective for many was to reduce expenditure.

Economic circumstances have, therefore, resulted in changes in the staffing structures of libraries. Moreover, the advent of systems like team

6

librarianship, themselves a result of the need to maximise the contribution of professional staff, means that branch libraries often do not have professional librarians available and library assistants have been promoted to supervisory grades (Russell, 1985). The delegation of important operational tasks to non-librarians requires they possess superior library skills, sound judgement and creativity to ensure a consistently high level of service (McCann et al, 1990). In these circumstances, managers now need to identify the best methods of ensuring their support staff learn to work in new ways and adapt to the new circumstances. New roles and relationships will entail a move away from the traditional way of thinking and organizing the human resources of library services, ensuring that all staff are equipped with the means to cope with change.

The management of change

Organizations are structures of opportunity and risk and people join them for a variety of different reasons including the chance to earn money, for prestige or because of the need to belong to something (Levine, 1984). In order to attract and retain high quality employees, an organization must strike a balance between the benefits it offers staff and the burdens it places upon them. An organization undergoing change, however, can easily fall into the trap of neglecting benefits while increasing burdens to make ends meet in the short term.

Management literature used to take a growth environment for granted and although the management of change has been a popular topic since the Second World War, 'change' invariably meant expansion. A 'growth ideology' led to a widespread belief among managers that growth is a sign of success, no growth a sign of stagnation, and retrenchment a sign of failure (Luce, 1983). This left many senior executives unprepared for recession. In the 1980s, however, the fact that retrenchment may be unavoidable was recognised (White, 1982), and over the last couple of decades, the language of 'cutback' has become increasingly prevalent with references to declines, cuts and contraction.

Organizational decline is a form of organizational change but the problems of managing change are compounded by a scarcity of resources (Levine, 1978). Moreover, unlike in times of growth, employees may be anxious that their jobs are at risk and their career development will come to a halt (Levine, 1984). All change - by definition - disrupts the working situation but in a retrenching operation the challenge for managers is how to prevent uncertainty reaching crisis proportions (Greenhalgh, 1982) as financial, morale, and personnel problems are layered on top of the usual administrative and customer service issues.

7

Although the general organizational literature has had few examples of decline, deletion, shrinkage, loss etc. as a central variable (Russel, 1989), studies of the effects of 'downsizing' and the best way of managing it are increasing in number. This literature of cutback management has a dual focus concentrating on the strategic decision responses to externally imposed cutbacks, and/or the potential and behavioural responses likely to arise out of cutbacks (Jick and Murray, 1982). Thus, the value that the firm attaches to human resources and their management are the principal issues that managers are learning to address as a result of downsizing (Appelbaum, 1991).

However, it has been suggested that while managers are becoming more adept at managing the technical side of strategic change, the human or behavioural side is still often neglected (see, e.g. Buch and Aldridge, 1990), although it is increasingly recognised that organizations that do not pay sufficient attention to how their employees are affected by management decisions are misguided and will eventually have to pay the price for their insensitivity.

As organizations adapt to hard times, employees may be subject to various forms of work-related stress including uncertainty, instability, insecurity, increased workload, role conflict and ambiguity, pressures to cut costs, and strains between management and staff. Employees may be attracted to their jobs because they like the tasks involved but dissatisfaction with other dimensions of their work may dampen overall satisfaction and cause distress (Wahba, 1978). There is also evidence that inadequate resources can adversely affect the attitudes and emotions of workers as well as their motivation because workers need personal, social and material resources to perform their jobs adequately (Katzell and Thompson, 1990). In short, it is a stress situation that is likely to contain many more demands and constraints than opportunities (Jick, 1985).

> Simply put, it just is not as much fun working and managing in a
> contracting organization as it is in an expanding one (Levine,
> 1979, p. 80).

Thus, the human or behavioural issues connected with change must not be neglected. Managers will have to orient their staff so that they have the skills and motivation to operate effectively in this new environment. The concept of quality assurance is also currently high on the management and political agenda. Good managers realise that the quality of staff response is crucial to customers' perception of a library or information service and will be concerned to ensure that their recruitment, selection, training and staff development policies reflect this.

8

Change, and its subsequent effect on the structures, staffing patterns, relationships and staff responsibilities in libraries, has focused increasing attention on library support staff, as the growing importance of paraprofessionals and library assistants for the smooth operation of services is recognised. Support staff are playing an increasingly crucial role in the provision of services as library and information organizations attempt to use their limited professional resources as effectively and efficiently as possible. Out of this process a new type of library worker, the paraprofessional, has emerged.

The research

The research upon which this book is based was a qualitative study of nine English local authority public library services (Goulding, 1993). One polytechnic library was also included as a control subject. Seventy five staff of all levels (support staff, professional librarians and representatives of the senior management team) were interviewed individually. All the direct quotes in the text come from the above study.

The basis for the study was that changing external and internal environmental conditions, some of which have been identified above, have affected support staff working conditions, attitudes and opportunities. A second proposition was that it is library managers' responsibility to be fully aware of the effect of these changes on their support staff and to intervene to promote the positive and ameliorate any negative aspects of change. The aims of the study were thus to:

1. identify, describe and assess the impact of internal and external environmental factors on support staff;
2. assess and analyse the quality of the response of library managers responsible for such staff.

Although the research was carried out in public libraries, many of the issues, problems and underlying trends are relevant for managers across the library and information sector. The challenge of managing change is universal across all types of libraries, and managers must be aware of how change affects the working experiences of staff, and how, in the face of uncertainty and upheaval, they can ensure those staff remain motivated and committed. From a management viewpoint, what will be of particular interest are the comments and observations made by the support staff, in their own words, when reflecting on their own positions and that of their library services, providing a rich picture of the current state of support staff roles in libraries.

Contents

The book is divided into two parts. Part I examines how changing internal organizational and external environmental circumstances have affected support staff in libraries. Chapter 1 explains who library support staff are, what they do and why there is increasing interest in their working conditions and attitudes to work. This chapter also includes a review of what this category of staff find satisfying and dissatisfying about their work. Chapter 2 examines the changing work environment for support staff, outlining how the changes described in the introduction have affected support staff in their work, concentrating in particular on how the changing climate has affected those aspects of work identified in chapter 1 as satisfying and dissatisfying.

Part II of the book reviews how management has, could and should respond in these circumstances and suggests strategies management can employ to cope with the above. Chapter 3 discusses work design and investigates the potential of various job design methods that managers could use to improve the working environment for their support staff. Chapter 4 examines working conditions and how management can try to positively influence aspects within the workplace such as job security, the physical working environment, career development and team working. Chapter 5 discusses the organizational climate and management strategies for ensuring support staff are kept informed and feel they have the support of their management. This chapter also includes an examination of training, and of organizational culture including an assessment of methods that managers might employ to try to change the prevailing culture of their library or information services so that it supports organizational goals. Chapter 6 concentrates on workforce planning and equal opportunities, including a discussion of the drive for flexibility and the implications of this for equal opportunities. The conclusions draw out some of the important issues that arise from the previous chapters and expand upon management's response to the emergence of this new type of support staff worker.

Part I
SUPPORT STAFF AND THE CHANGING CLIMATE

1 Support staff and their work

This chapter discusses the role, responsibilities and status of library support staff with the aim of providing managers with a better understanding of the nature of support staff work. Managers need to be aware of the attitudes of support staff towards their work, and the second half of this chapter is an examination of the job satisfaction of support staff, identifying the degree and focus of support staff job satisfaction and discussing the factors that can affect their motivation and morale.

Support staff are playing an increasingly important role in the provision of services as library and information organizations attempt to use their limited professional resources as effectively and efficiently as possible. Managers must identify the best way of ensuring their support staff learn to work in new ways and adapt to changing circumstances. First of all, though, managers need a thorough understanding of who their support staff are, what they do, and how they feel about their work.

Library support staff - who are they?

Library assistants have been described as "the invisible people" (Toolis, 1976) of the library world, attracting little attention from the public, their local authority employers or even their professionally qualified colleagues. Up until recently, Library Associations have similarly had little involvement with this category of staff who are so vital to the delivery of library services. Simply put, the library profession has not come to grips with, nor developed plans for, the education and efficient employment of this category of staff, the majority of library workers.

However, there does seem to be a growing awareness of the important role that library assistants play and the nature of the work they do and after many years of attracting only sporadic interest within the library and information world, support staff appear about to claim centre stage and become 'The issue of the nineties' (Timberlake, 1990).

Nomenclature and definitions

After long being overlooked, staff in 'non-professional' posts in libraries are suddenly finding themselves in the limelight, with two magazines now devoted to their interests and concerns, and courted by the Library Association to become Affiliated Members. The practice of enclosing the term 'non-professional' in inverted commas illustrates the problem many encounter with definition and nomenclature of this category of library and information worker.

Library assistants are collectively described as 'support', 'auxiliary' or 'ancillary' staff. Although the term 'non-professional' is still used in practice, ideally it should be avoided, implying as it does a lack of skill and competence. 'Non-professional' has negative connotations and gives the impression of a person doing low-quality work. Although the term is still heard in library services, staff are beginning to reject it:

> I like to be referred to as what I am, not what I'm not and I do think most library assistants feel that they're just as professional (and we're using a small 'p' now), as anyone on the staff; they just don't have a degree and a library qualification (library assistant, polytechnic library).[1]

There is an abundance of terms used to describe this large category of staff including library assistant, information assistant, senior library assistant, library administrator, library clerk, paraprofessional, subprofessional, library page, library media technical assistant, library associate, library aide and even career librarian, mini-librarian, nonlibrarian and support professional. However, there seems to be little rhyme or reason to the many titles given to these posts. It is often a matter of local preference.

Paraprofessionals

The term paraprofessional is now 'officially' used by the Library Association. 'Para' means:

> ...beside ... as in paramedical, helping doctors or supplementing medical work (Levett,1981, p. 47).

A paraprofessional is thus a trained aid who assists a professional person (Hofstetter, 1982) and paraprofessionalism is:

> ...the knowledge, use and understanding of a range of specific techniques, procedures and services that can be undertaken according to a set of predetermined rules, without the need to exercise professional judgement in decision making (Nettlefold, 1985, p. 7).

In other countries, most notably the United States, Canada and Australia, 'paraprofessional' is used to describe the second layer in a three-tiered staffing structure with professionals above and non-professionals (clerical staff, maintenance staff, security staff, etc.) below in recognition of the fact that library jobs cannot always be divided into two clear categories (Shields, 1988) and that a middle level staff can relieve professionals from the routines, techniques and procedures which do not require full professional training (Webb, 1990).

This higher grade of support staff normally undergoes some form of higher education leading to awards such as certificates and diplomas and generally supports librarians in providing information services and supervising other members of the support staff.

It has been suggested that the reason such a class of employee has not emerged here in Britain is due to the relationship between support staff and professional librarians (Russell, 1986) who fear that their skills will be down-graded or diluted and resent the claim on their 'exclusive skill jurisdiction' (Nettleford, 1989).

Defining the term 'paraprofessional' in a British context is problematic when there is no recognised library technician qualification as in North America, Australia and Eastern European Countries. However, what *has* emerged in most libraries, despite the absence of a recognised paraprofessional qualification, is a three-tiered staffing structure with professionally qualified librarians at one level, below which are senior support staff who supervise the library assistants below them.

Some library assistants have always undertaken semi-professional duties. As long ago as 1962, for example, a report of the Library Association Sub-Committee on In-Service Training acknowledged that,

> One thing that seems to emerge is that there is a considerable area of work which is sub-professional rather than non-professional (Sub-committee on In-Service Training, 1962, p. 174).

The emergence of this middle tier of staff has lately accelerated, or at least been highlighted by the recent structural and other changes identified in the introduction, so although it could be argued that there has always been a need to consider this group separately and to attend to the problems and concerns surrounding their working conditions, status and role, these issues now demand a more urgent investigation and solution.

The middle ranking library staff in the scheme outlined above are distinguished from librarians by having an operational role while librarians have a developmental focus. It could be said that paraprofessionals are decision takers but not policy makers.

The difficulty comes in distinguishing between the two support staff categories. Neither holds a professional qualification from a Library Association accredited course and yet those in the middle level deserve the title 'paraprofessional' and are distinct members of the library team. They are distinguished from their colleagues below them by being in supervisory, although not policy making, positions. They are the senior support staff, undertaking the more complex tasks and procedures, interpreting policy and implementing it on behalf of the professional staff.

Paraprofessionals can be distinguished from general library assistants by their role, duties and responsibilities rather than simply their educational qualifications, vocational or otherwise. The amount of supervision paraprofessionals give and receive would appear to be one of their main distinguishing features. Often they are in day-to-day charge of a service point and directly responsible to the area librarian. As well as the time-tabling of staff, many are involved in recruitment procedures, appraisal and training. Compiling the library's statistics and administering its paperwork is another area of work now the responsibility of paraprofessionals.

Typically library assistants' jobs are more repetitive, less complicated and require a more limited knowledge of practices and procedures. Library assistants thus carry out specific tasks which require little or no knowledge of related processes. They undertake the routine tasks and procedures of production work while the more complex tasks and procedures, needing some knowledge of the policies and the system which generate them, are the preserve of the paraprofessional.

Although it is the role and responsibilities that paraprofessionals undertake, as opposed to the possession of formal qualifications, which distinguish them from general library assistants, librarians *can* be defined in terms of their education and training. Henceforth, the generic terms 'support staff' and 'assistants' will be used to describe,

...those staff who have not taken professional examinations and who are not, therefore, chartered librarians nor studying for chartership (Scarrot, 1989, p. 16).

These are staff who perform library duties but do not have an Library Association accredited degree.

The more senior grades of support staff, the second layer in the three-tiered system described above, will be referred to hereafter as 'paraprofessionals' while the term 'library assistant' will be used to refer to those below them at the third level.

Value

Considerable attention is now being focused on library support staff and this new interest is partly the result of the external pressures on library services set out in the introduction. Although demands on services have often increased, there has rarely been a corresponding increase in the number of librarians on the staff. Thus, library services have adopted a 'coping mechanism' whereby paraprofessionals are increasingly being used to fill supervisory posts as well as in other complex library positions as economic pressures force services into using librarians only for tasks justified by their professional training and education (Clemens, 1983).

This task redistribution has significantly upgraded the level of work performed by support staff, and so there has been an increased recognition of staff at assistant level accompanied by an acknowledgement from practitioners that,

...if non-supervisory library workers were all to disappear the library would grind to a halt within a week at most (Toolis, 1976, p. 19).

Furthermore, customers' perception of an organization's quality is held in the hands of its people (Smith, 1990) and many users' opinions of their library service will be based as much on the treatment received from assistants as on the bookstock, especially as for many users, the library assistant is 'The Librarian'. Because they are often the first 'port of call' for library users and have the most contact with them, the importance of a happy, productive support staff is crucial.

Support staff satisfaction

Support staff are often positively drawn to library work and the types of duties performed in libraries. Table 1.1 gives a summary of responses of what the support staff in the study reported here found most satisfying about their work. As many other surveys have found (e.g. Estabrook et al 1990, Thapisa, 1989, Russell, 1986), the opportunity to work with books and people attracts many recruits to library work at support staff level.

Table 1.1
Satisfying aspects of support staff work

Helping or working with people	35%
Reference/enquiry work	7%
Colleagues	9%
Working with printed material	8%
Variety/unpredictability of work	6%
Promotion/advancement	6%
To see the end result of work	6%
Administration	2%
Other	10%

Working with the public

Contact with users is the main attraction of library work for support staff. As table 1.1 shows, the greatest appeal of library work lies in working with and helping people. The opportunity to work with a variety of users or to work with specific sections of the community, be that the social, academic or business community, can be immensely satisfying. Developing a bond with users, helping meet their leisure reading or informational needs, and appreciation for doing so, is very fulfilling for assistants. Being able to assist users with a problem, or help them find what they need often makes the job worthwhile.

Assistants perceive their work as significant to their organizations and their users and derive a high degree of job satisfaction from this service role. Day-to-day contact with users and their satisfaction with the service they receive leaves assistants feeling fulfilled. Although there can be very busy times when assistants are under a certain amount of pressure, work with people still gives them most pleasure and satisfaction. Contact with users is thus the most important focus of assistants' job satisfaction. Essentially, support staff derive satisfaction from being able to produce something that is actually needed by somebody else, be it a book, a report or a piece of information.

Enquiry work

Although the focus of support staff job satisfaction is contact with people, there are other facets of the job that are fulfilling, the opportunity to work with books being one of these. Assistants get great pleasure from being able to match people with the sort of material they need, and enquiry work ideally combines assistants' readiness to serve the public, with their inclination for working with the printed word.

Although the debate about whether library assistants should carry out reference work continues to occupy the attention of many in the profession, assistants find that answering reference enquiries is often the most rewarding part of their job. The opportunity of dealing with members of the public on a one-to-one basis and being able to answer their specific queries is generally much more satisfying than working on the circulation desk, issuing books and doing other routine library housekeeping duties. Assistants enjoy the more interesting side of information work and welcome being at the forefront of the service, facing the users and fielding any questions they might throw at them. Those working on information desks seem to especially enjoy the unpredictable nature of their jobs:

> Here, I like the actual information work on the desk because you never know what's coming next. It's so interesting and it exercises your brain. You never know what the next question is going to be and it's a nice feeling if you can help people (library assistant, county council).[2]

Again, the crucial element is the chance to help people find the information they need, either just general local information or especially more specialised data. 'Task significance' is thus vital to the job satisfaction of library support staff, i.e. staff feel their work is meaningful because it has an effect on the lives and work of other people (Hackman and Oldham, 1980).

Co-workers and colleagues

Although this contact with the general public is very motivating for support staff, other interpersonal relations can also be a significant source of satisfaction. The importance of good relations with work-mates and the pleasure of working with congenial colleagues is crucial for a happy and productive working atmosphere. In jobs which lack deep inherent satisfaction, good working relationships are often crucial to the maintenance of motivation and morale. Senior library assistants, or paraprofessionals, can also gain great satisfaction and pleasure from staff administration and supervision. As their staff supervision responsibilities increase, a major part of their role is to help other staff with any problems they may be encountering either at work or outside. These training, counselling and team-building responsibilities are personnel duties that paraprofessionals often find particularly fulfilling.

Variety and unpredictability

It has been suggested that the reason support staff have largely been ignored in the profession is because much of their day is taken up with the essential, but routine, housekeeping duties of circulation, filing and shelving. Support staff insist, however, that public library work is not all routine:

> Although people think libraries are quiet, there's never a quiet moment here (paraprofessional, London borough).[3]

For those outside the library field, the idea that the job of a library assistant is often unpredictable and varied may come as something of a surprise. However, although a lot of the housekeeping work in public libraries is the same every day, the pace and order of duties is quite erratic and can come in 'fits and starts':

> I don't know what's going to happen each day. I mean, I know you get the set routines but you don't know what's going to come in through that door, what problems, and that's what adds the interest to it and that's what gives me satisfaction (library assistant, metropolitan borough).[4]

Variety in work is highly prized and the opportunity for employees to undertake a variety of duties in their work and use a number of different skills is another important component of employee job satisfaction (Hackman and Lawler, 1971).

Promotion

Career opportunities for support staff will be discussed in more detail in the next chapter, where it will be suggested that organizational change has not been accompanied by corresponding radical adjustments to the reward systems of many library services. The chance to advance, working their way up from being a library assistant to supervising their own branches, can be immensely satisfying for support staff. Perhaps because assistants recognise the limitation on their chances of advancement, those who do rise up the ladder appreciate it all the more:

> Well, I've progressed, about one of the only people that have. There's not many that have because there's no career structure, but I progressed from a library assistant, part-time. I suppose that's quite satisfying; progressing (paraprofessional, London borough).[5]

Knowledge of what support staff find satisfying about their work can help managers positively influence their working environment. This should be accompanied by an effort to discover what assistants dislike about their jobs too, so that an attempt can be made to reduce any stressors that may be having an adverse effect on performance.

Dissatisfaction

The collective results of most surveys of library assistants generally show that they are most dissatisfied with the monotonous nature of their work as well as the lack of promotion possibilities, and their relations with the professional staff (e.g. Butler, 1983).

Table 1.2
Dissatisfying aspects of support staff work

Unable to think of anything dissatisfying	21%
Inability to provide as good a service as they would like	17%
Workload	14%
Lack of promotion/advancement	14%
Routine procedures	10%
Management	6%
Pay	4%
Difficult customers	4%
Other	9%

However, as table 1.2 shows, only the second of these featured prominently in the study reported here when support staff were asked what they considered the most dissatisfying aspect of their work. One of the most remarkable features of this aspect of the study is the number of assistants who could not think of anything they found dissatisfying.

Inability to satisfy the public

If assistants' job satisfaction derives primarily from being of service to the public, it follows that when they believe they are not doing this adequately, they will not feel fulfilled. Assistants often feel that they are unable to fully satisfy users' demands, and find this disturbing and distressing. Lack of resources is often blamed:

> I feel that we haven't got enough staff to be able to do our job to the best of our ability really. I feel there is so much more that we could do if we had more staff (paraprofessional, London borough).[6]

Assistants experience considerable frustration when they cannot satisfy people's requests and often despair of the rising number of customer complaints and their services' inability to offer more services:

> You're continuously struggling to just achieve the basic running of the department. I never actually have the time to sit back, look at the department and look how you can improve. And if you do have ideas how to improve you're never able to carry them out. It's just lack of time (paraprofessional, London borough).[7]

Assistants generally enter library work because of the desire to work with people but often find that dealing with demanding and dissatisfied users dissipates their satisfaction with this aspect of their work. Providing a good quality service engenders a sense of pride and achievement and a feeling of having accomplished something personally believed to be worthwhile or meaningful. Unfortunately, shortage of resources, materials and staff, means that support staff can lack this feeling of satisfaction. Staff shortages are also blamed for increasing assistants' workload.

Workload

The amount of pressure this extra burden of work imposes is another major dissatisfying aspect of assistants' jobs which is ascribed to lack of emergency cover, as well as staff shortages. As noted above, this causes considerable frustration when it means assistants cannot satisfy the public's needs:

You want to spend more time with [members of the public] but you're always conscious there's somebody else waiting, and you've got other work to do as well (library assistant, metropolitan borough).[8]

Understaffing can lead to backlogs and queues. The image that untidy shelves and long queues present to the public is a worry, especially at a time when customer care programmes are being adopted by more and more library departments:

We even have trouble controlling the shelving. It's pretty demoralising when you see the shelving piling up. It does look bad, and we feel bad, but there's nothing we can do because it takes a lot of staff to man this library (library assistant, county council).[9]

Staff can feel overburdened by the amount of work they have to do and the rate they are expected to produce it. Although contact with the public is the most satisfying part of support staff work, it can become stressful if they feel they are not responding satisfactorily (Hodges, 1991).

Lack of promotion prospects

The limitation on their promotion opportunities features prominently in support staff gripes about their jobs. As noted in table 1.1 above, the opportunity to *advance* was mentioned as a *satisfying* aspect of support staff work. However, as table 1.2 shows, the *lack* of opportunities to advance also is a major *dissatisfying* factor. Lack of career and promotion prospects is the focus of much support staff discontent and frustration. Assistants reach the top of the support staff career ladder and are frustrated that their hard work, long service and experience is not rewarded by a promotion because of the restrictive nature of the grading structure.

A number of public and academic libraries have introduced career grades for support staff, often enabling them to move on to scales which overlap with those of professionally qualified librarians. However, while library assistants acknowledge these efforts to improve their prospects, they also make the point that these more senior paraprofessional posts are few and far between. The problems and issues surrounding the subjects of promotion and grading will be discussed in greater detail in later chapters but it is important to note that opportunities to advance are an important source of satisfaction with both the organization and the individual's job. When they are lacking, employees can feel betrayed and confused.

Pay

The prospect of promotion opportunities, along with pay rises, are perhaps the two most tangible means of reward open to managers hoping to increase the motivation of their staff. Pay is a complicated motivator because the actual amount in the wage packet at the end of the day is not necessarily important. More significant may be the items that can be purchased with that money, or the degree of status and self esteem the wage represents for the individual. Inadequate salaries have been found to be a great source of discontent among library assistants (Thapisa, 1989).

However, in the interviews conducted for this research, although assistants spoke at considerable length about their pay when asked about it directly, it was rarely identified as the *most* dissatisfying aspect of their jobs. Nevertheless, this does not mean that library managers should be complacent about wages. Library staff of all levels often feel very strongly that support staff pay is:

> Abysmal! For the hours we work and the responsibility, and the time that I've been here, I think that it's shocking and I sometimes wonder why on earth I stay (paraprofessional, county council).[10]

Routine duties

If the poor wage does not persuade staff to leave, then perhaps the predictability of library work might. Few relish the prospect of tedious work, and a lack of challenge can provoke apathy and disaffection. The limitation on the extent to which the job requires paraprofessionals to use their education and abilities has the potential of causing considerable dissatisfaction (Russell, 1986). However, in the study reported here, dissatisfaction with the monotony of routine procedures did not feature heavily. In fact, routine duties can be a restful respite from busy periods, giving staff time and space to recover. Assistants appear to accept routine duties as just another part of their job, acknowledging that all jobs have their routine elements.

Management

Support staff can value routine, then. Indeed, change, and the way it is handled can be unsettling and worrying. In sensitive times, managers have a dual role to play: to protect staff; and to change the working atmosphere for them if it is not conducive to maintaining morale (Hardy, 1987). Even when staff are fully aware of the reasons for organizational change and have been informed and consulted, they are still generally wary of it. Restoring some sense of direction for staff, and re-establishing high morale and keen motivation are key management functions in times of change (Imberman, 1989). To restore a positive working environment after or during change, the manager must establish a dialogue that clarifies employees' concerns (Jacobs, 1988). Unfortunately, this dialogue between senior management and staff on the ground is not always initiated, or sustained in times of pressure, leaving staff unsure about their prospects with the library service.

Conclusions

Many of the day-to-day tasks support staff perform are not inherently interesting or likely to inspire enormous excitement which could be a factor in explaining the previous comparative lack of attention given to the everyday experiences of this category of library staff. However, the development of their role means that the profession must now attend to some of the complex issues surrounding them, e.g. their status, training and career opportunities, working conditions and responsibilities. It is library managers' responsibility to be fully aware of how the changes outlined in the introduction may have impacted on their assistants' working conditions, attitudes and opportunities and their overall satisfaction. Assistants form the bulk of the library workforce and managers must make an effort to acquaint themselves with the nature and characteristics of this important section of their staff and their attitudes to their work.

Notes

1. Goulding, A. (1993), *Managing Public Library Support Staff in Times of Change*, p. 4
2. Ibid, p. 94
3. Ibid, p. 93
4. Ibid, p. 93
5. Ibid, p. 96
6. Ibid, p. 103
7. Ibid, p. 103
8. Ibid, p. 102
9. Ibid, p. 103
10. Ibid, p. 144

2 The changing work climate

This chapter will discuss how the changes outlined in the introduction have affected support staff in their work, including an assessment of the impact on those aspects of their work they find satisfying and dissatisfying as outlined in chapter 1. This analysis will be divided into three sections:

- the nature of support staff work, i.e. the challenge, responsibility, autonomy and variety involved in their day to day jobs;
- their working conditions and environment, e.g. job security, physical working conditions, pay and promotion;
- the organizational climate, including management style, training and organizational culture.

The nature of support staff work

As the introduction explained, changes in staffing structures have led to a trend whereby fewer, more tightly organized professional librarians are supported by increasingly skilled assistants who now have more supervisory duties as well as responsibility for tasks and areas of work once considered 'professional'. Chapter 1 outlined how key supervisory positions, for example, once the preserve of librarians, are now held by paraprofessionals. This enlargement of the support staff role will have had an effect on the intrinsically satisfying nature of their jobs, especially on the responsibility, challenge, autonomy and variety in their work.

Responsibility

Responsibility is one of Herzberg's 'motivators' (Herzberg et al, 1959), necessary to give work meaning and satisfaction. 'Responsibility' can either mean the accountability assistants have for other individuals, their co-workers; or it can refer to the aspects of work in the library support staff are responsible for, their duties.

Which ever way the word is interpreted, it seems clear that assistants' responsibility has increased with alterations in staffing structures and the subsequent redistribution of tasks and workload this has caused, combined with budgetary restrictions:

> Far less money progressively over recent years has meant that we're probably asking more of non-professional staff. It's been an evolutionary thing; they've been taking on more and more, even if it's been because of the accident of having less professional time to put alongside them. The general and senior library assistant is becoming far more a rounded individual in terms of skills (senior manager, metropolitan borough).[1]

Reduced staffing levels are often the driving force behind the trend for support staff to take on more, and more responsible, tasks. The declining numbers of professional librarians, and the demands on the time of those remaining, has created the need for support staff to take over some of their tasks. The burden of the tasks and duties that librarians have relinquished to their support staff has fallen primarily onto paraprofessional shoulders but this can have a knock-on effect on the library assistants they supervise as the senior support staff delegate some of *their* responsibilities to those below them.

However, the duties of the senior support staff members have undergone the greatest transformation. This category of staff is aware of the increasingly responsible nature of their posts and, in recognition of this, new positions have been created with titles such as library manager or library administrator.

These more senior grades of support staff have varying degrees of responsibility, but most now have more service point administration and staff supervision duties. These paraprofessionals can be described as possessing 'intermediate level skills', i.e. higher than semi-skilled but lower than full professional level. Recent research for the Employment Department confirms that employees with intermediate skills are becoming more important in the workplace (Rolfe et al, 1994). They free professional staff for specialised work while providing a skilled supervisory layer for unskilled and semi-skilled assistants.

Restructuring has thus transformed the nature of operational level supervision. This has resulted in an increase in the number of functions paraprofessional supervisors fulfil and the range of responsibilities invested in them.

Broadly, these roles can be categorised as follows:

- work scheduling and allocation;
- security, housekeeping and maintenance;
- training and development of staff, including recruitment and appraising;
- people management including communicating, motivating, team-building, and maintaining discipline.

The first-line supervisor's role is of vital organizational importance. These employees are a key resource with a definite and critical role to play in the workplace, developing and training those under their control and translating management's plans and policies into action. They are uniquely located at the interface of management control and operational level, where management's plans are implemented. Paraprofessionals also play an important role in communication, often have responsibility for decision making delegated from management, and have a crucial co-ordinating function in teams.

As indicated in chapter 1, support staff gain a high degree of job satisfaction when their duties cross over with those of the professionally qualified staff e.g. enquiry work, and there are benefits for the library in this as it encourages staff to use their initiative and abilities for the good of the service as a whole. However, managers could be accused of exploiting their support staff if they are not paid a proper rate for the job, and it could also create a distorted image in assistants' minds of what professional work encompasses.

Challenge

Extra responsibilities may not necessarily prove more satisfying unless they challenge the employee's skills and abilities so that they feel they have produced or accomplished something of consequence (Hackman and Lawler, 1971). To gain challenge for their work support staff should be involved in activities that test their skills and knowledge.

Once again, reorganizations of library staffing structures and budgetary changes have often had a positive effect on the job content of support staff jobs as professional staff numbers are rationalised and overall staffing patterns reviewed and modified. The trend towards organizing library staff along team structures has resulted in more operational tasks being delegated to support staff. As assistants undertake many of the tasks once considered the preserve of the professional librarian, the challenge of their posts increases. This frequently results in higher job satisfaction:

It's harder, the job's harder, but I find it more satisfying. I was never one to turn down a challenge (paraprofessional, London borough).[2]

This challenge is often found in learning to use and in operating computerised library systems. Although there is a danger that IT can over-simplify work, with less opportunity for individual initiative, in libraries, increased computerization tends to increase job complexity and the decision making potential of support staff posts (Gattiker and Howg, 1990). New technology can make assistants' work more varied and interesting by dispensing with much of the paperwork drudgery of their tasks. As libraries acquire more and more pieces of technological equipment, staff have to learn to use them and exploit what they offer to the full. As a result the range of tasks and complexity of the assistant's job has increased:

We now have systems that are computerised and require quite a degree of flexibility, common-sense, intelligence, a mixture of all those things. I mean I'm not saying that old manual systems were particularly straightforward and easy to use but there are certain barriers that have to be overcome in terms of using machinery (senior manager, metropolitan borough).[3]

Managers must be careful, however, that the pressure and demands made of the more senior support staff do not rise to an unacceptable level as they take over more of the administrative tasks once done by librarians. At its worst, this can result in a production line environment where opportunities for independence, creativity and autonomy are limited:

Pressure, having to deal with things a lot more quickly, although I don't know if I'd use the word 'challenging' (paraprofessional, metropolitan borough).[4]

There is also the danger that this pressure combined with financial constraints will encourage libraries to abandon plans for an expansion of services, leading to support staff reverting to largely routine work. In this situation staff can feel disheartened by their positions and lack of opportunities to use their skills and knowledge to their best advantage. However, new services, largely the result of the new media and information technology available in libraries, are being developed, increasing assistants' workload but also enlarging the range and complexity of skills they need to use.

Autonomy

A production line environment can also mean that staff are rigorously time-tabled with little freedom to structure their own working day or to decide what they do, when and how. Changes in staffing patterns in libraries, however, often mean that the degree of autonomy support staff are allowed has increased as reductions in the number of professional librarians employed has resulted in more distant supervision.

The personality and working methods of the assistant's line manager determines how much opportunity for independent action an individual is allowed but, at paraprofessional level in particular, radical changes in the level and type of work undertaken has been accompanied by high degrees of autonomy. Paraprofessionals are now given considerable freedom to run their sections or service points as they see fit. On a daily basis, these senior support staff do not have the sense that they are being strictly directed, although there are clear limits to their independence:

> Small things I can decide on. Major things I always have to go to the area manager. Anything to do with money, I have to go to her (paraprofessional, London borough).[5]

Those on lower grades, though, often feel rigorously time-tabled. The increasingly workload and tight staffing resources mentioned in chapter 1 plays its part in this because time becomes too limited to allow assistants to take the initiative. If assistants are required to undertake extra counter or shelving duties because of a lack of emergency cover, the degree of freedom they have to schedule their own work is obviously drastically reduced. These restrictions can also limit the amount of variety in support staff work as there may be no relief staff to allow the assistant on the issues desk, for example, to attend to other duties.

Variety

As suggested in chapter 1, variety in work is much appreciated by support staff. The development of new services, as libraries respond to the changing needs and demands of users by diversifying their service offerings, has had the effect of increasing the number of operations support staff are now required to undertake, the variety of equipment they use and the procedures they perform.

Changes in staff structures have also played their part in increasing the variety of support staff work but perhaps the most important influence is the use of new technology. As argued above, the deskilling effects of IT have been overemphasised and although it has been suggested that new automated library systems bind assistants to the issues desk, restricting interaction with users and limiting opportunities to experience other aspects of library work (Davis et al, 1991), new technology can provide assistants with the chance to do more, rather than less:

> We used to have to check manually for all reservations; we used to write all the tickets out whereas now it's simply the one plastic card. We did find at first, in some cases, we didn't have quite as much to do, but there are other things to do at the counter now (library assistant, metropolitan borough).[6]

Computerised circulation systems demand new skills and provide different types of information which assistants can access. This is not to deny that assistants have always had quite varied work but new technology has relieved them of some of the very routine work which can now be done automatically, filing library tickets, for example, or issuing overdue reminders. However, whether the automatic procedures which have taken their place are more interesting or not is a matter for debate.

Nevertheless, although the type of work support staff is now involved in may be quite similar to the sort of administrative work they have always been responsible for, the number of duties they are expected to undertake has increased considerably.

Working conditions

Although most recent work in the area of motivation has concentrated on the importance of the intrinsic aspects of job satisfaction discussed above, few employees would deny the importance of contextual factors like workload, physical working conditions and job security (Gruneberg, 1979). As chapter 1 points out, a pleasant, sociable, constructive working atmosphere is important for library support staff but changing environmental conditions has had a significant impact on these aspects of working life.

Workload

An increasing workload is a major source of dissatisfaction at work for library support staff, the result of restricted staffing caused by prolonged economic stringency and uncertainty. Frozen posts, vacancies and lack of emergency cover all increase the workload of support staff retained after any restructuring. Staff often feel there is more work to do than time to do it and, in public libraries, as service points and hours are reduced to save money from the staff budget so there is less time for dealing with the same, or increased, workload.

Those at service point level are intensely aware of increasing pressure to do more with less. Staff reductions combined with absences and frozen posts can compound an already difficult situation:

> They haven't refilled jobs when they became empty so the staff that are left are put under a lot of stress and strain (library assistant, metropolitan borough).[7]

Libraries have diversified their service offerings in an attempt to meet new user demands but this increasing range of services is not always accompanied by extra staff to administer them. Although staff enjoy seeing their services grow and develop, new services can thus also be viewed as extra pressure especially if they feel that their attention is spread so thinly it is having a detrimental effect on the quality of the service they provide the user.

Quality of service

Chapter 1 emphasised the importance of user satisfaction for library support staff. Assistants show considerable commitment to serving their clients, but there is an almost equally strong sense of frustration that they are not able to provide an adequate service.

Concern about the quality of service provided to users is heightened by increases in customer complaints about the stock and service. Ashamed not to be providing the level of service they once did, assistants can become dispirited and suffer a serious decline in motivation and morale as they observe customer expectations falling. They resent having to offer a substandard service and bear the brunt of customer complaints as it is usually the support staff who are in the users' firing line. Staff dealing with users on a day-to-day basis feel that their ability to respond in a satisfactory manner has been severely curtailed by financial pressures. The increased workload mentioned above, for example, means that staff are unable to spend as long as they would like with individuals.

Staffing restrictions are commonly blamed for a perceived decline in quality:

> We've tried to keep the quality of our service up as far as possible. The only restrictions we've had really are staff shortages. If there's only one person on, then obviously if there's a crowd of people in you can't give the amount of attention you'd like (librarian, metropolitan borough).[8]

There is concern that contracting staffing levels will tell on the service's quality of response, and a perception that these restrictions have had an effect on individual assistant's ability to respond to users' needs in a satisfactory manner. A perceived reduction in the time available to devote to each individual patron is regarded as affecting the quality of service provision for the worse by making it much less personal:

> We are more hurried now. We've got to get a lot more things done and a bit more quickly so you're not spending as much time with each person as you'd like to (library assistant, London borough).[9]

The lack of time to give users the attention they deserve and to pursue matters to a full and satisfactory conclusion can make work less enjoyable for assistants although they remain determined to provide as good a service as possible in sometimes very difficult circumstances. In fact, the emphasis on customer care as part of the drive for quality described in the introduction, has often improved the response of library staff on the ground and has increased the standard of service delivered:

> If you were measuring [quality] in terms of the personal service [users] get from the library assistants, it's gone up, partly because we're more aware of how important public relations are, partly because we train them more now and partly, I think, because they know they've got more responsibility and they have reacted to that (librarian, county council).[10]

Support staff also feel that the instant access to information provided by computers has improved the service they offer to their users, although there can be problems with overloaded and slow systems which increase the tension in staff/user relations and put assistants under quite a strain.

The increasing range of services available as libraries stock different types of media and offer new services to attract new users and respond to the demands of existing ones is also considered to have added to the quality of service although, as noted above, budgetary restrictions can be a serious barrier to innovation. Nevertheless, extra facilities are seen as improving the service offered to users and are considered a marketing tactic to attract more customers or retain the faithful.

However, increasing the number and range of services at a time when library budgets are not growing means that managers have to manage their resources much more rigorously. There is concern that libraries are trying to spread themselves too thinly and the book fund is bearing the brunt of this.

Reductions in the book fund are perceived as having a serious impact on the stock and the service provided to the public. Once again, the staff with the most public contact, i.e. the support staff, have to deal with any complaints.

Support staff feel a degree of responsibility on two fronts. They have a deep commitment to providing their users with the best possible service, and also a sense of responsibility to their own library service, to support what it is trying to do in uncertain times. However, job satisfaction can be undermined as they witness expectations of the service declining.

Physical working conditions

The physical quality of the book stock can also give assistants cause for concern, as can the physical repair and general appearance of the library environment. Chapter 1 noted that support staff often feel that the sheer volume of work means that their essential housekeeping duties of tidying and straightening shelves are sometimes neglected.

The increasing workload can also mean a more physically demanding job. The popular image of library work as undemanding and sedate is a myth as far as support staff are concerned:

> People tend to think of working in a library as a very easy sort of job. They say 'Oh, I wouldn't mind doing that, a nice little job', but actually it is quite a demanding job. I don't think people realise just how physical, and how heavy books and reference materials are (library assistant, county council).[11]

Adverse environmental conditions, especially poor air quality, noise, ergonomic conditions and lack of privacy can affect worker satisfaction and mental health (Klitzman and Stellman, 1989). Economic stringency and lack of ready cash can means that broken equipment may not be immediately replaced and there is inadequate provision for the decoration, maintenance and repair of premises:

> There's no doubt about it, we're slower to replace equipment, furniture, the decor is terrible in some cases. Our ability to actually spend money on repairs and maintenance which should be done for safety reasons is only just about there, so the luxury of painting an area of plaster to make it look nice is just that: a luxury (senior manager, metropolitan borough).[12]

The support staff working in these conditions can become dispirited with having to make do and mend, but generally, the main dissatisfaction arises out of not being able to make improvements rather than out of a massive decline in the situation.

Job security

Job security has become a major consideration in the last few decades which have witnessed frequent periods of high unemployment. Uncertain about the future, many organizations have tried to streamline their operations and news of job freezes and budgetary constraints provoke anxieties among staff about the security of their jobs. There is also a trend towards employing more people on temporary contracts and on other flexible patterns such as on a part-time basis. In these cases, job insecurity does not just refer to the fear of being made redundant, but also to concern about losing certain valued aspects of their work.

Today, library support staff do not believe they are guaranteed job continuity. Although they may not worry that they are going to lose their jobs, they are anxious about losing certain aspects of their jobs or about their jobs changing in some way that would be detrimental. The restructuring taking place in many library organizations can lead staff to fear for their positions and the content of their jobs:

> We don't feel particularly secure. It's not just security in the job, of keeping our jobs, because we know we're going to keep our jobs for the next few years at least, because no-one else can do them basically, but as time goes on they will try and take bits of it away and the job satisfaction and the security in what we're doing is important as well (paraprofessional, London borough).[13]

A sense of control over job content and methods is an important element in job security for library support staff. A loss of influence over what their job entails, where they do it, and how it will effect their career prospects can engender a feeling of helplessness, so although few may feel their actual employment is under threat, they do worry that their positions will change in a deleterious way.

Pay

It seems reasonable to assume that the pay of library support staff will, these days, reflect the greater responsibility and complexity in their jobs. Library organizations have often introduced more progressive pay and grading structures which allow assistants to advance up the career ladder and earn at least as much as beginning librarians, and in some cases more.

Nevertheless, assistants still frequently feel underpaid, believe that the considerable increase in responsibility and duties in their posts should be appropriately rewarded, and that their current wage does not in any way take into account the extra duties they have taken on and the new skills they have had to learn. Support staff have noticed a huge change in the complexity and amount of work they undertake but feel that the reward system remains pitifully inadequate.

> I think we're low paid considering the fact that we're in charge of all our banking, not budgeting as yet, but the amount of paperwork we're asked to do, security of the building. We're only paid on a clerical scale whereas we're actually in fact managers and responsible for buildings (paraprofessional, London borough).[14]

Although commentators in the library and information world fear that support staff will compare their wages with those of their professionally qualified colleagues, leading to conflict and division between the grades (Veaner, 1982), more often assistants compare themselves with workers outside libraries, and, in public libraries, with other local authority workers in particular:

> The person receiving the same pay as me would be a Repairs Reporting Clerk for the Housing Department, sitting at the end of a phone with a computer screen in front of him or her, and get the same pay as me. I have thirty staff and a building this size so I feel aggrieved (paraprofessional, London borough).[15]

It has been suggested that library assistants will never be paid their due because librarianship, especially the lower ranks, is dominated by women and so subject to inequitable compensation (Johnson, 1987). In libraries, this horizontal segregation of the workforce is accompanied by vertical segregation as promotion prospects are much better for the male worker. While female professional librarians may protest about the 'glass ceiling' effect which means that they can often rise no further than middle management positions, library assistants are faced with the more tangible obstacle of often only having two grades to progress through.

Promotion

Although, as mentioned above, library organizations have often modified their staff structures in ways that allow for more paraprofessional promotion, staff still feel that opportunities for library assistants to advance up the career ladder have not improved significantly despite the fact that their job responsibilities have enlarged. Despite the blurring of professional and support staff tasks, and the consequent resentment often felt by paraprofessionals over prospects and rewards, few want to become professionally qualified, but they do want a fulfilling job and one that offers some opportunity for promotion.

Today, low turnover, frozen posts and declining establishments, the results of budgetary constraints, exacerbate the difficulties faced by library assistants eager to take on more responsibility and progress up the career ladder. Structural changes to enhance career prospects for support staff are limited by organizations' difficulties in finding the cash to meet any wage rises accompanying up-grading.

In uncertain economic times fewer staff are likely, or able, to take the risk of leaving or moving. This causes a bottleneck in the organizational hierarchy as library assistants reach the top of their pay scales but have little prospect of a higher graded paraprofessional post. Declining staff numbers have also led to a decrease or, at the very least, a stagnation in the number of vacancies:

> A lot of jobs have been lost. There's much higher competition for the jobs that are left and the range of cuts have taken out whole levels of staff, so there's much less opportunity (paraprofessional, metropolitan borough).[16]

Mobility

At a time when opportunities for promotion, and the broadening of experience and chances for creativity it brings, are contracting, managers may consider other methods of maintaining the interest and motivation of staff. As noted above, variety in work is highly appreciated by support staff. The opportunity to use an assortment of different skills and engage in a spectrum of tasks can increase challenge and motivation. However, in situations of tight staffing the scope to do this is not always available. The lack of managers' time to attend to these matters is another problem which limits assistants' mobility around their organization:

I think if we had more of them and less other pressure to keep our libraries going in a certain direction, I'd be able to look at each assistant and be able to assess what he or she wants. That's where the barrier comes. If I had the time to do that I could give them the opportunity of going elsewhere, trying out different places but although the opportunities are there, they have to go and get them because I just don't have time (librarian, London borough).[17]

Working relations

As the previous chapter indicated, a major source of job satisfaction for library support staff is their contact with their co-workers. Social opportunities and interaction with colleagues is of more importance to assistants than professionals who find their greatest source of satisfaction at work in factors related to their duties. Restricted budgets, though, can lead to conflicts among colleagues as competition for status and resources intensifies. Irritable or negative work-mates and gossip arising out of anxiety about the service can be a source of considerable stress (Bunge, 1989), and personal antipathies are likely to emerge in times of low mobility when there is more competition for rare internal promotion. In times of pressure, with staff under increasing strain and anxious about their job security, co-operation can decline and individuals refuse to exert more effort than they need to, or fail to pull their weight:

Everybody's digging their heels in and drawing the line at not doing more than they should be doing whereas normally they'd be quite happy to help out (paraprofessional, London borough).[18]

However, there is a chance that low mobility and difficult circumstances can contribute to a good working atmosphere. Staff are able to build up relationships, and team spirit and loyalty are encouraged in the face of adversity (Pankhurst, 1984):

We probably work more as a team now. I think because there's so few of us we have to know what each other's doing. Whereas before you could be more of an individual if you wanted to, now you really have to pull in as part of the team (paraprofessional, London borough).[19]

The same could be said of relations between support staff and professional librarians. The changes in staffing structures, along with alterations in the ratio of professional to support staff, has the potential of heightening the risk of conflict between the two categories of staff, especially when there is little movement within the profession. However, restructuring can have a beneficial effect on the relationship between professionals and support staff as communication between different section and levels of staff increases and the demarcation lines between professional and support staff tasks are less defined. This can bring a better mutual understanding of respective roles and as a consequence co-operation and understanding is strengthened as the need for everyone to pull together in any crisis that might arise is recognised.

Organizational climate

The need for management to sustain a healthy organizational climate is especially important in times of rapid internal and external change. It is management's task to effect the context within which staff work and attempt to improve the work environment for them. Unfortunately, in any organization undergoing change, staff management can be difficult. The organization may be in turmoil with crisis management prevailing over a broader, long term perspective. In these circumstances, managers, concerned to reduce overheads, meet budgets and save money, may inadvertently push employee concerns down the list of priorities (Hardy, 1987).

Feedback

Giving staff some indication of how they are performing in their new roles and how they are coping with their new responsibilities is essential after organizational change. Staff need to know how they are doing in their restructured jobs, how they might improve, what is expected of them and what they can expect in return. Feedback may be especially important for paraprofessionals in the wake of restructuring, many having taken on a considerable increase in responsibility. Unfortunately, line managers can be so concerned with performing adequately in their own jobs that they forget the needs of those below them. On the other hand, the closer working relationships brought about by restructuring may have made it easier for managers to tell their assistants when they have worked particularly well.

The information network

In times of organizational change, employees' need for information about the organization increases. Anxiety caused by knowing the organization is in flux is exacerbated by ambiguity about how management will respond. Some of this anxiety is caused by the lack of contingency plans, some by the limitations on communication that are inevitable in a crisis-ridden organization, some because of the deliberate withholding of information on the part of management who mistakenly believe secrecy to be wise during uncertain times (Greenhalgh, 1982).

The importance of keeping staff informed of the changes occurring and how it will affect them cannot be underestimated. Although library managers often go to considerable lengths to keep employees up to date with developments, the need for confidentiality over sensitive issues means that staff can still feel they do not know what is going on to a large extent. Crises and uncertainty can encourage secrecy and a decline in co-operation among the various parts of an organization, and pressures of time and workload may mean a decrease in interaction. In these circumstances the unofficial communication network comes into its own, leading to rumour and hearsay:

> Of late, the communications from the top downwards has got
> very lax and we hear usually just through the grapevine before
> we actually get an official memo around (paraprofessional,
> London borough).[20]

Although complex communication structures are in place in libraries, these systems can fall down in times of stress with the result that support staff do not have a very clear idea about the way in which their department is managed. More crucially, they often hear about changes which involve them in a roundabout manner.

Consultation

The encouragement of free communication among all library staff members can have multiple benefits among the support staff. As well as furthering their self-esteem, it can strengthen morale, improve the quality of performance, and encourage them to develop a deep sense of loyalty to the library (Muller, 1965). In times of change, though, centralisation often occurs in an attempt to facilitate speed and efficiency of decision making. Uncertainty might tend to make library managers cut across the consensus approach and take increasing responsibility upon themselves.

On the positive side, the restructuring that many library services have undergone, and the subsequent enlargement of the support staff role, has promoted a constructive dialogue between support staff and their professionally qualified colleagues:

[The professional librarians] ask our opinion more. We haven't really got professionals like the old way. You used to have your librarian, then your deputy librarian, then just your ordinary assistants. That's gone out of the window. They do ask our opinion more, and they're more approachable (paraprofessional, London borough).[21]

It is particularly important to let employees air their ambivalence over change which can generate feelings of anxiety, fear, concern, expectation and anger. Staff 'on the ground' may feel that their managers are out of touch with the day-to-day problems they have to cope with and although staff recognise that the management is also under pressure, the opportunity to talk at less formal levels is often appreciated (Jacobs, 1988).

Training

The training budget often suffers disproportionately when cuts have to be made and in uncertain times there is a temptation to concentrate on survival to the detriment of staff development. Lack of time and money can mean that training opportunities are few and far between as organizations suspend training department operations. Funds for courses and conferences are squeezed at the very time that staff development is crucial to prepare the more senior support staff for their new enlarged managerial responsibilities, and to give assistants in general the confidence to tackle their new duties with assurance.

In fact, far sighted library employers have increased training opportunities for their support staff as they are coached to take over many of the administrative, staff supervision and public duties once undertaken by librarians. There is a greater awareness of the need for support staff to feel they are performing competently in their jobs, arising from the recognition that they have an important role to play in their libraries, along with a realisation of their expanding job descriptions.

Nevertheless, despite the good intentions of management, difficult financial circumstances can cause a reduction in training opportunities, not only because training budgets have been targeted, but also because management is distracted by other issues demanding their attention. The lack of time, both for trainers to train and for assistants to leave their posts to be trained, can be a major obstacle facing the individual eager to learn new skills or update existing ones:

It's the time factor really and the pressure of the work. As far as I'm concerned, personally I'm failing my assistants in their

41

training but I don't have the time to be available to train them when they're both in, and I can't call them both in outside their normal hours because it means I lose their hours elsewhere (librarian, county council).[22]

Pressure of work and inadequate staff numbers leave many desperately trying to keep up with new developments without regular training. Special problems face those in small and one person libraries where staff know cover will have to be drafted in to keep the service point open and may feel guilty, or reluctant, to put their employers to such trouble. When resources are tight employees may feel loath to ask for time off to attend expensive courses, nor do they want to leave their work colleagues short-staffed.

In times of economic stringency, attempts to enhance prospects by attending library school or even higher education college are also severely hampered. Not only are authorities reluctant to release the staff member and the necessary finance, but there is no guarantee of a permanent post at the end (Shields, 1988).

Organizational culture

Changing economic, political and social priorities demand an imaginative response from organizations which must adapt to new environmental conditions if they are to survive. Changes of leader and leadership style, growth, contraction and reorganization can alter the cultural norms in the organization. Whatever the changes are, major or minor, they need to be consolidated into the fabric of the organization. However, the prevailing culture can prove very tenacious. Various factors like staff roles and structures can work together to reinforce traditional cultural patterns, especially if staff feel any change is for the worse.

Today's organizations are committed to promoting the values of enterprise, quality, and customer service, and libraries are no exception. Although libraries should always be responsive to their community of users, that community can be very demanding and put unreasonable pressure on staff. On the one hand, libraries are expected to have a greater diversity of services and, on the other, the delivery of that service is expected to be quicker, more efficient and 'value for money'. It is often felt by staff of public libraries, for example, that their users have had the concept of customer service 'drummed into them' so that they now expect a high level of service as a right. Of course all library users should receive a good quality service, but the current climate encourages them to be very demanding, perhaps unreasonably so given the economic difficulties faced by organizations and institutions. This 'customer service generation' is much more critical, assertive over its rights and much more likely to question policies and decisions. The support staff, being on the front line of the service, are likely to bear the brunt of any complaints or grievances.

Another aspect of the 'Enterprise Culture' already mentioned in the introduction, is the encouragement of the public sector to raise money. These issues can be a matter of conscience for staff who often enter library work because of their sense of public duty and commitment to the underlying mission and ethos of libraries. Whether working in a public, academic or special library, support staff often have a deep faith in a service which exists to meet the needs of the whole of their community of users and endeavours to make information freely accessible to all. They may feel there has been an alarming tendency to dismiss these principles as unrealistic in the present climate (Govan, 1988) and worry about the change in the character of the service.

Conclusions

Inhibiting situational constraints can reduce performance and have a negative effect on employee satisfaction (O'Connor et al, 1984). Organizational change inconveniences employees who try to cling to whatever stability still exists. In this situation, commitment to the organization may weaken and staff can become less willing to make the short term sacrifices necessary to advance general organizational goals (Greenhalgh, 1982).

It is crucial that in these circumstances managers maintain organizational commitment among their staff. The commitment and dedication of support staff to their job is unquestionable but it can be severely tested when the organization is under pressure. Employees may experience a sense of betrayed loyalty. Declining staffing levels and the commensurate rise in workload for support staff operating service points can contribute to this feeling of betrayal if management appear unconcerned or ignorant of the stress and strain staff 'on the ground' are under. Trying to maintain services with limited resources can test the loyalty of the most committed. Combined with the upheaval of reorganization and restructuring, support staff can feel confused, anxious and overburdened by their duties and by the rate of change. A lack of consultation and communication can compound the feeling of support staff that they are unimportant in the scheme of things, as can the feeling that they are not being rewarded or appreciated for the extra effort they are expending.

A manager can look upon changes in the organization's internal and external circumstances with either gloom and alarm or with determination and excitement. If considered totally negatively, the organization's employees often suffer low morale, frustration, stress and a decline in productivity. If, on the other hand, limited resources are viewed as a chance for creativity and tackled pro-actively, the organization may reap the benefits of increased motivation, less duplication of effort, reduced overheads, discovery of untapped or under-utilised resources, elimination of low priority (perhaps unnecessary) services and organizational renewal (Lippet and Lippet, 1984).

As far as libraries are concerned, restructuring and the devolution of some management level responsibilities to support staff can strengthen organizational commitment and be considered an opportunity to reassess responsibilities, tasks and systems (Jones and Jordan, 1987). Support staff have reacted to the changes taking place in their libraries and within their own positions with remarkable equanimity. Many perceive a chance to improve their positions and jobs in the wake of restructuring. Management now has to devise structures and methods of working which will take advantage of their staff's enthusiasm while still ensuring continuity and the pursuit of organizational objectives.

Notes

1. Goulding, A. (1993), *Managing Public Library Support Staff in Times of Change,* p. 212
2. Ibid, p. 246
3. Ibid, p. 249
4. Ibid, p. 240
5. Ibid, p. 413
6. Ibid, p. 264
7. Ibid, p. 115
8. Ibid, p. 311
9. Ibid, p. 314
10. Ibid, p. 318
11. Ibid, p. 119
12. Ibid, p. 124
13. Ibid, p. 131
14. Ibid, p. 153
15. Ibid, p. 154
16. Ibid, p. 178
17. Ibid, p. 193
18. Ibid, p. 194
19. Ibid, p. 193
20. Ibid, p. 440
21. Ibid, p. 416
22. Ibid, p. 506

Part II
MANAGEMENT RESPONSE

3 Work design

Part I discussed how the changing climate has affected support staff in their work. The nature and focus of support staff job satisfaction was examined, and ways in which this might have been affected by changing environmental circumstances were outlined. This chapter identifies ways in which managers can structure the work of their support staff to incorporate more 'satisfiers' and ameliorate the effect of those 'dissatisfiers' considered.

For many, work is the major source of satisfaction in life (Chwe, 1978). Most people between the ages of 20 and 60 spend a large proportion of their waking hours at work and it is beneficial for both the organization and the individual if employees working eight hours a day, five days a week, enjoy their jobs. Employee satisfaction is, after all, a prerequisite to customer satisfaction (Smith, 1990). Low morale can reveal itself in high absenteeism, high turnover and an increasing number of customer complaints. Although libraries are not run for the benefit of the staff they employ, dissatisfaction with work can have a knock-on effect on the quality of service provided to the user.

Those nearer the top of the organizational hierarchy are theoretically taken to have higher levels of job satisfaction because of their capacity for discretion, prestige and chances for advancement (McNally, 1982). However, it is the support staff in libraries who are dealing with the public on a day-to-day basis, and, bearing in mind the importance of contented staff to quality customer relations, their satisfaction should be of the utmost priority.

Work design

Work design attempts to simultaneously satisfy both human and organizational goals through the manipulation of job characteristics (Buchanan, 1994). Quality, flexibility and responsiveness in meeting customer requirements are needed in an increasingly competitive climate, and work design encompasses organizational strategies which are concerned with increasing the quality of working life for support staff and, at the same time, with organizing work more flexibly and more efficiently (Hales, 1993). Work design thus aims to,

> ...change the design of work to enhance employee need satisfaction and to improve work motivation and performance (Buchanan and Huczynski, 1985, p. 71).

In order to do this, managers first need to clarify what makes their support staff satisfied and dissatisfied and so come to a better understanding of what motivates their employees to provide a quality service. As chapter 1 indicated, library support staff can gain a high degree of job satisfaction from their work. The fact that, in the study reported here, 21% of assistants could think of nothing they found dissatisfying about their jobs suggests that there are high levels of satisfaction.

Although some common themes do emerge from a discussion of library support staff job satisfaction, generalisations like these can be accused of being imprecise because of the essentially individualistic nature of job satisfaction and the importance of variables like the individual's personality, beliefs, attitude and expectations. Thus, it is important for library managers not just to acquaint themselves with the job characteristics that lead to general job satisfaction and dissatisfaction in support staff positions, but they should also make an effort to acquaint themselves with each individual member of their team. Only then can they attempt to create a working environment which the employee will find rewarding and satisfying and which is effective in the delivery of services. Principles of job analysis can be useful here.

Job analysis

Job analysis is a commonly used tool in human resource planning, specifically in the recruitment stage when it is used to clarify the nature of the job to be filled. Job analysis is the process of collecting and analysing information about tasks, responsibilities and the context of jobs, but some of the stages in the job analysis process could be used to gather information about how individual employees feel about their work in general and especially about individual tasks within their jobs. Information about job content, working conditions and working relations could be particularly important. For example, in the area of job content, data about tasks, duties, level of responsibility, the importance of the tasks performed and how often they are performed could be useful. The manager might also want to gather information about the job holder's physical and social environment, whether s/he work alone or with others, and what salary and other benefits the job commands.

Various methods of gathering this type of information are possible and the information will be more reliable and useful if more than one method is used. Employees could be asked to write a self-report or fill in a questionnaire. Group interviews are another possibility and are often fruitful ways of holding a discussion as employees in similar positions can 'bounce' ideas off one another. The critical incident technique can also be used to great advantage by asking employees to recall particular times when they felt good and bad about their work. Employees should be given the responsibility to analyse their own jobs and develop more efficient and effective ways of performing them.

Once managers have gathered information relating to the job satisfaction and motivating potential of jobs and particular tasks, they can then takes steps to try to positively influence the working environment for their staff.

Job rotation

Job rotation involves moving people around on a regular basis. It is a useful and commonly used way of trying to bring variety into jobs. As noted in chapter 1, variety is an aspect of work highly valued by support staff and remembering the maxim 'a change is as good as a rest', cross-training in other parts of the library can help bolster morale by allowing individuals to function in alternative capacities.

The benefits of gaining work experience in various sections of the library service are manifold. Assistants get the opportunity to develop a particular skill like children's work or information work, and it frees them from being behind a counter all day.

Job rotation can also enhance organizational efficiency and flexibility as it provides cover for absenteeism and enables the organization to redeploy workers from slack to busy areas in response to workload fluctuations. So as well as benefiting the individual, job rotation can provide the library with a pool of workers skilled in various different areas. It can also give support staff a better overall picture of their library service and where they fit into the organization. As an example, users complaining to an assistant on the circulation desk that a book they have reserved has not arrived are likely to receive a better informed response if that counter assistant has some knowledge of the reservations department and its procedures. Involving support staff in this way will not only give them more of a sense of what the library is about, but will also encourage them to see themselves as part of the organization and so increase their organizational commitment.

Thus, staff learn what other departments do and how they operate and this can help them do their own jobs. The library has a reserve of assistants with some practical experience in various departments, who know what the different jobs involve and whether they enjoy that type of work. Assistants sometimes feel that their knowledge of library work and what their service does is limited and would like the opportunity to move around:

> We don't see things like the mobile. I have been at the teachers' centre and I have been to branch libraries but I've never been to headquarters, to bib services or anything like that so I've never seen the cataloguing side or the background side to it. I feel that it might help in some respects to get a slightly broader picture (library assistant, London borough).[1]

Rotation aims to relieve monotony by offering some work variety. However, it does not always involve changes to job content or methods. The individual is often still doing essentially the same job, just in different places. The work assistants do as they rotate must be methodically planned and provide intellectual stimulation as well as variety. There is a danger in libraries that assistants are moved to different departments just because an extra pair of hands is needed:

> There's an amount of 'You will go and work in this section because it's needed' not 'You will be trained in this area or that area because it might enhance your job opportunities' (paraprofessional, metropolitan borough).[2]

The experience and training assistants receive in such circumstances is of questionable benefit.

The psychological comfort of assistants must also be attended to. For some, the disadvantages of moving to unfamiliar territory outweigh the perceived benefits and they do not want to move around. They have built up a good working relationship with their colleagues and users and resent being taken out of that environment and having their routine disrupted. It must always be remembered that individuals are often happier and perform better in certain roles so while some assistants are very good at working on the enquiry desk and like the demands that type of work makes on them, others are apprehensive of taking on such responsibilities and prefer contact with users just at the issue desk or may even feel more comfortable undertaking backroom duties. While recognising that there is a need to give people

50

variety of experience and a full view of the service, management must be careful to use individuals' strengths and talents as best they can, and where they feel most comfortable:

> My personal feeling is that I like people to move around because I think it's good for experience but having said that you have to recognise that a lot of people do not like change, they find it threatening and it saps their morale; they're worried about it. So you've got to balance the need for giving them wider experience, giving them variety with the need not to scare them, give them a sense of belonging to a place (senior manager, metropolitan borough).[3]

Not all staff want to experience new environments or processes and should not be forced into a situation in which they would feel ill at ease or incompetent.

Finally, the logistical problems of a large scale job rotation programme should not be overlooked. The lack of time and staffing resources to extend the opportunity to rotate to all assistants is a major stumbling block. Taking just one person out of their normal working environment for even a short period can cause serious disruption to staffing patterns and time-tables. Furthermore, managers are often too hard pressed to pursue these opportunities for their support staff. A successful job rotation programme needs the attention of one member of staff, preferably of a senior capacity, who can monitor progress, systematically draw up a programme and schedule, and take some of the burden of the administration from line managers. The programme should aim to give assistants experience of user and technical services, and, in academic and public libraries, of small and large sites.

The benefits of mobility around the library are many, but staff should not be randomly allocated on a week-by-week basis to different service points. The continuity of familiar faces is important for users, and staff also need some stability. It is important to remember the informal social relationships which everyone builds up and which, as noted in chapter 1, are a major source of satisfaction with work for support staff. To move people around as if such relationships were of no consequence is bound to lead to feelings of frustration and dissatisfaction (Gruneberg, 1979). Too many and too frequent moves can be unsettling and decrease commitment as the individual has little time in which to develop the job or the necessary skills to perform it efficiently. Job rotation can also take an inordinate amount of time which many libraries may not have the luxury of setting aside.

Job enlargement

Both job rotation and job enlargement offer relatively simple, cheap methods of trying to make the work environment more satisfying. Job enlargement means adding other tasks of the same level to a person's job, again, usually to prevent boredom. Here, the manager would be adding to the number of operations an individual is expected to undertake, in order to make it more interesting. Again, this job design method is essentially concerned with adding variety to employees' work. The opportunity for individuals to undertake a variety of duties in their work and use a number of different skills is an important component of job satisfaction (Hackman and Lawler, 1971). The changes to library staffing structures set out in the introduction have had the effect of increasing the number of operations support staff are now required to undertake, the variety of equipment they use and the procedures they perform. As outlined in chapter 2, the introduction of new services, and particularly the increasing number of pieces of IT equipment have been important aspects in the increase in the variety of support staff jobs.

Job enlargement is often referred to as horizontal loading as it adds to the number of tasks at the same level and the technique has been criticised because of this. Merely increasing the number of unskilled tasks performed is not in itself likely to add very much to the challenge of the job (Gruneberg, 1979). Job enlargement could involve just adding more boring tasks to the boring tasks already undertaken and so has been accused of adding little to the challenge of the job or to the development and growth of the individual, and of simply meaning the employee just does more work.

Traditionally, library assistants' jobs involved a range of tasks including filing, looking up catalogues, issuing and returning books, etc. While few of these tasks may have been intrinsically interesting at least they required a degree of physical effort and permitted some interaction with co-workers and library users. In contrast, new automated library systems, for example, may bind an assistant to the issues desk with little opportunity to experience other aspects of library work and restricting interaction with library users and colleagues. Although assistants desire variety in their posts, if the various tasks have little coherence or individuals lack a sense of purpose, job satisfaction will be minimal.

Job enlargement is easy to introduce and to a certain extent is happening anyway for support staff in libraries but because of the perceived deficiencies of job enlargement, library managers should aim not just to increase the number of tasks undertaken but also to ensure those tasks constitute a full cycle of work. This is known as job enrichment.

Job enrichment

Job enrichment is often referred to as vertical, as opposed to horizontal, loading. This method increases the variety of tasks undertaken but also involves giving the job meaning and challenge. The tasks added should be of a more interesting or demanding nature and should give employees extra responsibility for planning, monitoring or controlling certain aspects of work. Job enrichment occurs when significant elements of discretion and self-supervision are added, with the employees given the opportunity to plan their work sequence, choose their work methods and tools, allocate their time and monitor their output (Hales, 1993)

Job enrichment is closely linked with the theories of Herzberg (Herzberg et al., 1959). The aim is to add job characteristics which are 'motivators', i.e. a sense of achievement, responsibility, recognition, opportunities for personal growth, and intrinsic work interest. Job enrichment should be motivating because it should stretch the individual who should have a greater sense of accomplishment, a better attitude to work and better relationships with subordinates and superiors.

Skill variety

In libraries, job enrichment for support staff has come about to a certain extent through restructuring. Senior library assistants in public libraries, for example, are now responsible for service points and all the extra duties and responsibilities that go along with that. Support staff now often have greater discretion in setting schedules and work methods and checking on the quality of work and training of those below them. The important difference between the variety implied here, and the mere growth in the number of tasks undertaken as characterised by job enlargement, is that the various activities allow the individual to use a number of different skills. Support staff who feel that their work demands a lot of their various talents, skills and abilities are likely to feel their job is worthwhile.

To gain this sense of challenge, support staff should be involved in activities that test their skills and knowledge, and restructuring with its attendant task reallocation has made this a reality for assistants. The need to make full and efficient use of human resources also means that everybody who works in the library who has a skill, whatever its nature, utilises and exploits that talent to the full for the good of the service. Efficiency and flexibility arguments for job enrichment are thus just as important as those concerned with assistants' quality of work life.

Managers must be careful, however, that the pressure for the former does not lead to the neglect of the latter and that unreasonable demands are not made of support staff. Attempts to reduce the professional staff establishment and delegate some of their tasks downwards as a way of making more efficient use of professional expertise, can have a positive effect on the job content and therefore job satisfaction of support staff. It can also cause stress:

> [Assistants] certainly find [the work] harder. It's harder physically in that you do more work per capita, and I think it's harder intellectually. Because we expect them to do more, and the whole system has become more complicated, they can't do it in a sort of zombie-like sleep which we've all done a bit on counters in the past. I think some of them enjoy the challenge (senior manager, county council).[4]

Presumably some of them do not. Nevertheless, although extra duties can increase pressure, it is also possible that they can enrich jobs, providing assistants with new challenges (Hall, 1982) and more stimulation and interest. As the amount of effort expended increases, so there is a corresponding rise in the sense of accomplishment. As long as the amount of work an individual has is not exhausting, an increased load can stimulate higher levels of satisfaction with work (Miller et al, 1990) and the opportunity to do work of a more demanding or intellectual nature is often appreciated by assistants:

> When I first started we had professional librarians who did all the brain work and we just shelved and tidied and did all the boring things but I get quite a lot of paperwork and behind-the-scenes work now (library assistant, county council).[5]

Thus, despite the increase in pressure identified above and in part I, the satisfaction that support staff derive from their jobs has also grown, although this has generally occurred because of the necessity on the part of library service to restructure their staffing establishments rather than through the desire to increase the meaningfulness of work for their support staff:

> I'd say we had a very open view about what [support staff] can do. I mean one must be cynical and say it's all really to get more done for less money but the benefits aren't bad, do you see what I mean? The reason behind it perhaps is pretty sour, that we're always trying to do everything on an absolute shoestring but for the library assistants themselves I think it's had spin-off benefits (senior manager, county council).[6]

Managers can capitalise on the results of restructuring, whatever the impetus driving it, by taking the opportunity to carefully examine support staff roles, responsibilities, capabilities and aspirations in order to identify how and where their jobs can be enriched. One area that should be reviewed is the degree to which they are able to do a whole piece of work.

Task identity

As noted in chapter 1, task identity is an important part of job enrichment. This refers to the ability of each employee to do the whole or entire job so that in the end s/he is able to identify with the results of their efforts (Thapisa, 1989a). If individuals are responsible for a specific duty or aspect of work and its outcome (successful or not), then it is easier for them to clearly identify the result of their efforts, thus giving their work meaning and satisfaction. Task fragmentation, on the other hand, can lead to frustration and boredom. Jobs should be designed so that each member of the work group can perform a meaningful and properly bounded segment of work for which s/he can fully 'own' or be responsible for. Each task should be a sufficiently whole piece of work so that the individual can, in the end, identify a worthwhile outcome (Hackman and Lawler, 1971).

It is important to give library assistants specific areas of work which they feel are their responsibility, in fact, everyone in the library should have 'ownership' of one particular activity (Line and Robertson, 1989). In situations of limited staffing, though, this policy can provoke resentment if the individual has her/his own particular area of work to attend to but has to abandon it because of the need to undertake more pressing, but more routine duties. Managers may also be reluctant because of the need to keep the staff flexible, in which case specialisation would be avoided. Library support staff enjoy having their own specific area of work for which they are responsible, although this might seem to conflict with their desire for variety. In fact, although assistants value the opportunity to engage in different duties and type of work throughout the day, they also appreciate having an area of work they can call their own. Allowing support staff control over a whole process or task enables them to identify with the end product.

Table 1.1 in chapter 1 shows that being able to see the result of any work they may do gives library assistants high levels of satisfaction. To some extent, it does not matter which part of the service the assistant works in as long as s/he can follow through a whole task, e.g. an assistant in a reference section will feel greater satisfaction if s/he is able to do all the work relating to an enquiry themselves and then hand the result to the user, rather than merely doing one or the other.

However, assistants' sense of being able to clearly identify the ultimate aims and results of their work is often lacking:

> The very nature of the work means that it has to be structured so it is very much interleaved with a variety of activities and therefore actually seeing an end-point or conclusion is quite difficult in that job, and it is quite difficult to structure work so that individuals actually perceive their own contribution to the end (librarian, London borough).[7]

Being involved in projects right from the beginning and seeing them through to a successful conclusion can be immensely satisfying for support staff. This might be easier for paraprofessionals who now play a larger role in planning, and are able to follow a scheme through from the inception of an idea to its implementation. Even for library assistants, though, the ability to do a whole piece of work is important although the situation of tight staffing, which many libraries are operating within, means that just getting a job done can be reward enough. Clearing a backlog or completing a task can be a satisfaction in itself, although this kind of high pressure environment is unlikely to inspire much creativity or give staff time to reflect on the outcome of their work. Support staff can feel at the mercy of the system and their various tasks can lack coherence and thus meaning. A sense of purpose can be achieved by assistants, though, if management makes the importance of their role quite clear.

Task significance

Chapter 1 suggested that job satisfaction for library support staff is predominantly service-oriented but that this sense of service can often be disappointed or lacking, particularly in times of crisis when staff have little time or inclination to reflect on the value or worth of what they are doing. Management can help by establishing clear connections between an individual's work and its value to the user so that staff may experience a sense of self-confirming service and recognition (Jones, 1984). Involvement in all the operational aspects of running the library can help in this respect:

> It's a service industry and they see the importance of that, they see the importance of helping people, the purpose of the library. They're not just numbers, they're not just the scale 3 who comes in from 1 - 5 or whatever, they're there to help people and unless they're all involved in everything and can see the direction of the

library and their part in it then they'll have no job satisfaction and the library would go downhill rapidly (librarian, London borough).[8]

Managers must communicate the importance of the support staff role for both the service outcomes and the organization and articluate that assistants form the backbone of library operations and play a major part in the continuity and stability of services. This can be helped by structuring work so that the employee can perceive that s/he has produced or accomplished something of consequence. Support staff take a pride in giving excellent service and contributing to a high quality product. Giving them the opportunity to function in various capacities will help convince them of the essential functional and operational role they play in their library as well as the importance of their public relations role for their libraries and authorities (Taylor, 1981).

Enabling staff to function in various sections of the library and so understand the nature of the service and its importance as an operation can thus help convince staff of the value of their work. Managers must also capitalise on any positive messages from users to give staff a sense of the importance of their jobs. One way managers might consider to increase assistants' sense of personal achievement and worth is to allow them more independence and responsibility in the workplace.

Autonomy

Autonomy is the extent to which employees have a major say in what they do at work, how they do it, when, and what equipment they will use. Under these conditions employees are more likely to feel personally responsible for their work and 'own' its outcomes, so experiencing a feeling of personal success and rise in self-esteem (Hackman and Lawler, 1971).

Chapter 2 explained that change has increased the amount of autonomy experienced by paraprofessionals as they are now in day-to-day charge of service points and have little close supervision. For library assistants, however, the opposite has often occurred as tight staffing means that they have to be strictly time-tabled, and have little say over what they do, when and how.

The opportunity for support staff to structure their own working day varies enormously, and is very often dependent upon the personality and working methods of the librarian in charge or that of the senior support staff supervisor. Library assistants on the lower grades in particular feel that their work is strictly organized and distributed by others and there is little flexibility in what they do or how they do it. Their duties are generally laid down and there is a standard method of doing them. The nature of library work means that strict time-tabling is often essential and there are certain routines which have to be done on a regular basis. Although there may be a degree of consultation between library managers and assistants about task allocation, the cyclical nature of library work means that there is generally not a great deal of freedom.

In organizations made up of many individual units, a certain amount of control is inevitable and desirable to monitor quality, ensure all are fulfilling the aims of the service and to impose a degree of uniformity among service points. However, there does seem scope for allowing support staff more autonomy. Although there are a number of tasks that have to be completed by the end of the day in any library service, the sequence and priority given to those duties can be the responsibility of the staff, and often are in more relaxed organizations. Even when there are certain duties that need to be completed, and even in a particular order, there is still scope for discretion:

> There are various aspects of work that I have to do, but if I finish my job I can go and say 'Right, what do you want me to do next? Can I do this? Shall I do that?' So I have a fair amount of freedom, I don't feel restricted in any way. I feel that I'm allowed to see where there's a necessity and I can fill that gap (library assistant, county council).[9]

Although the human relations school of organizational psychology has emphasised the importance of autonomy and responsibility, for library assistants, being free of tight supervision by substituting adequate guidelines is satisfaction enough (Jones, 1984). Support staff are generally satisfied with their freedom to make decisions regarding their own jobs within quite a rigidly structured framework. They recognise that there is a core of work that has to be done every day and as long as they have a certain amount of freedom to organize their working day and the chance to become involved in projects that are of particular interest to them, they accept that they have to work to a time-table.

Managers may, however, wish to increase the autonomy of their assistants. Cost cutting has forced managers to place greater trust in their support staff as their own workload has increased sharply. This means they must increasingly operate through self-managed teams and self-directed individuals. Reluctance to take on increased responsibility may be an obstacle, though:

> I'm quite happy with the freedom that I've got and I wouldn't particularly want more freedom to make other decisions in the post that I've got (library assistant, metropolitan borough).[10]

As layers of management are reduced, organizations will increasingly rely on the commitment of staff and their willingness to take control of their own working lives. A balance does need to be struck, though, between freedom and control and this can be difficult, especially in large dispersed organizations. Autonomy does not mean giving people the freedom to do as they choose. Everyone must operate with strict regard to the achievement of organizational goals. Staff should be involved in the process of deciding what controls they think they need. Above all they need guidance. Support staff need to understand organizational goals, how they contribute to them, what exactly is the purpose of their job and the constraints and limitations surrounding it. They need to know what has to be accomplished and they need to be aware of the requirements and limitations of their roles, schedules and time limits. They should be given general guidance rather than specific direction (Kinlaw, 1995).

Support staff may initially be wary or apprehensive of operating without strict instruction and one way mangers may consider easing assistants' anxiety is to create a more limited, safer environment in which their autonomy can operate by first delegating greater freedom to teams.

Autonomous work groups

In larger systems, teams of support staff responsible for particular service points are practically self-governing. The members of these teams possess a variety of skills and are accountable for operational decisions relating to production, control and scheduling. They are also responsible for co-ordinating with other teams within the system and with the rest of the organization. More and more management roles and functions are being given to teams, often as a result of structural changes. They typically work towards goals set with their managers but they organize their own work and control and monitor their own performance. The support staff in these teams share a close sense of membership with their colleagues and they share responsibility for providing the day-to-day service to their users.

Teams are becoming the preferred way of making use of the mental resources of people. They provide a structure for delivering whole projects and managing processes from the beginning to end. All existing work groups present the opportunity for team development but in libraries, although teams do have a degree of autonomy, there is scope for extending this. On a daily basis team members do not have the sense that they are being strictly directed, but they are still aware that there are limits to their independence. Although it is imperative that service priorities and long term strategic planning are safeguarded, the teams delivering the service to users should be allowed as much freedom as possible over their own working practices and procedures. Doing the job every day, they are the people who know the job best.

There is a risk of stifling individual or group enterprise by making every decision subject to approval by a higher authority. Although a degree of direction is necessary, teams could be given 'defined' autonomy, a type of closed freedom determined by specific directions, limitation and checks on performance (Kinlaw, 1995). They could, for example, in consultation with their managers, set their own targets for their unit within the overall organizational goals, and establish their own performance standards. Teams stimulate higher levels of energy to address issues and have the opportunity to take advantage of the knowledge, skills and experience of each member. It is also an unthreatening arena in which to test ideas and opinions, especially for those staff who, because of their place in the organizational hierarchy, are not used to being involved in planning and goal setting.

Conclusions

The broadening of assistants' roles, responsibilities and skills gives managers the opportunity to take a serious look at what is now expected of support staff and the way they are expected to perform their jobs. Managers need to ensure that employees have the opportunity to take advantage of the shift in roles and functions. The unavoidable requirement to work more efficiently, with fewer human resources and at higher levels of quality means that organizations must find ways of discovering the hidden talents and competence of support staff, and then developing methods of enhancing those skills and maximising their use for the good of the library and its users.

The word 'empowerment' has become a popular term for:

> The process of achieving continuous improvement in an organization's performance by developing and extending the competent influence of individuals and teams over the areas and functions which affect their performance and that of the total organization (Kinlaw, 1995, p. 21).

Initially this means giving staff greater influence over the individual tasks associated with their jobs which in turn necessitates a reduction in supervision and regulations and training in new skills such as problem solving. Support staff in libraries are empowered to some extent already but there is a need to extend what already exists to ensure they have maximum control over their jobs by finding opportunities for them to apply the full range of their skills and experience. This requires structural changes in the

60

way teams are organized and managed, and systematic changes like shortening lines of communication.

It also involves a change of attitude on the part of both managers and staff. Employees may not at first appreciate the opportunity to manage themselves and their work. Used to working in bureaucratic hierarchies, staff are often ill-equipped to become more self-reliant. This can be a liability when organizational conditions demand greater flexibility and adaptability, but until support staff are given the opportunity to demonstrate their capacity for greater responsibility and self-sufficiency, they will never know themselves what they are capable of, and neither will management be able to tap the full extent of skill and experience at its disposal.

As support staff take on additional tasks, responsibilities and accountabilities so they are becoming increasingly responsible for managing themselves and yet, as stressed above, not all staff want to become 'empowered'. Not everyone dislikes repetitive jobs and, from time to time, employees may appreciate the chance to 'switch off', to daydream and to think about other aspects of their life. The opportunities for this for today's library support staff seem limited, however, and the often highly demanding nature of the work has implications for the recruitment and selection policies of library services. Newcomers must be able and willing to accept responsibility and, in the meantime, existing staff must be equipped and perhaps persuaded to do so.

Support staff might very well question how they benefit from taking on greater responsibility and accountability at a time when ongoing cutbacks have reduced the workforce and may continue to do so. Managers have to make it clear that staff are being given the opportunity to make the best use of their skills and resources by allowing them to act to the full extent of their potential both as individuals and as far as their jobs are concerned. The chance for increased recognition and development can be an important motivator, especially at times when there are limited opportunities for movement or promotion.

Support staff should be encouraged to make decisions for themselves, initially perhaps decisions relating directly to the operation of their individual job like scheduling their own working day. This can immediately generate a sense of influence and control which can be built upon until collectively the support staff of service points are organizing, controlling and monitoring all the work of their unit, deciding what their goals are and how they will be achieved. For managers, this means relinquishing power and trusting people. It also entails accepting that staff might make mistakes and appreciating that making mistakes is part of learning. It involves giving support staff the responsibility for the outcome of the service on the ground and the support and authority to take the service in the direction they choose, within clear limits, and then being prepared to let them do as they see fit (Lee, 1994).

If managers are willing to trust support staff by taking advantage of new organizational structures and theories of job design, it is possible that they will be more committed to, and accepting of, change. In this scenario, rather than seeing change as something to be feared, they see it as an exciting opportunity to extend their influence.

Notes

1. Goulding, A. (1993), *Managing Public Library Support Staff in Times of Change,* p. 188
2. Ibid, p. 195
3. Ibid, p. 199
4. Ibid, p. 242
5. Ibid, p. 270
6. Ibid, p. 214
7. Ibid, p. 107
8. Ibid, p. 97
9. Ibid, p. 420
10. Ibid, p. 422

4 The working environment

Spurred on by European Community social policy, organizations have recently been paying much closer attention to health and safety at work. Although still predominantly focused on the prevention of workplace accidents, employers are nevertheless becoming increasingly sensitive to other employee concerns including violence, sexual harassment and stress. The importance of a working atmosphere which is conducive to quality work from all staff should not be under-emphasised. Effective management of the work environment can enhance employee commitment and play a major role in the quest for Total Quality Management (Bach, 1994).

This chapter discusses various aspects of the working environment and suggests how management might establish a working atmosphere conducive to good performance, focusing specifically on:

- workload and physical working conditions;
- conditions of work, specifically job security, pay and promotion;
- working relations, with users and colleagues.

Working conditions

Workload

Chapter 1 noted that workload was a major dissatisfying feature of work for support staff who feel that the amount of work they have to do has increased quite dramatically, declining staffing levels being the reason most often cited. Staff reductions combined with shorter opening hours mean that staff often have a higher workload but less time in which to complete it, leading to a high pressure environment. Absences and frozen posts can compound this already difficult situation. Generally, staff can cope as long as everyone turns in for work but if the library is not fully staffed, the situation can become very pressurised.

Although declining staffing levels are perhaps the most obvious causes of an increasing workload, other factors must also be taken into account:

> We have fewer members of staff but jobs still have to be done so [support staff] do seem to have to work perhaps harder than they did in the past and that means stress. What we find here also is that although issues are going down, we are developing other services like videos and we're trying to attract people into the libraries in other ways, so in actual fact, with fewer people, we're perhaps asking them to do more (librarian, London borough).[1]

A greater emphasis on income generation can also mean that assistants have more work to do but within the same number of hours, and the introduction of different type of media and diversification of services can similarly increase demand and thus pressure.

As well as a quantitative overload of work, support staff are also in danger of being qualitatively burdened. Staff shortages can mean more work for everyone but this is potentially more serious for support staff if they have to cover or take over the work of a professionally qualified librarian. The transfer of 'professional' tasks to support staff and the possible positive effects of this process have been discussed in previous chapters, but managers must not be complacent that all the outcomes are beneficial for the employee. Roles change and role expectations often multiply as increased output is demanded of fewer staff. Staff can feel overwhelmed as they attempt to adapt to the added job functions, new relationships and even new surroundings which often follow reorganization (Jacobs, 1988):

> We [support staff] are expected to do more, supposed to do more work with the same amount of people, sometimes less people, which has you running around wearing four hats at a time (paraprofessional, London borough).[2]

This role ambiguity can result in employees feeling less involved in their work and so less inclined to exert as much effort towards providing a high quality service. Individuals may find themselves developing into Jacks or Jills of all trades if a number of people in the section leave and they are given responsibility for all their various tasks as well as their own. Job fragmentation can also occur as employees lose the sense of obvious relationships between tasks which form their job (Thapisa, 1990). Workforce planning and flexibility will be discussed in a later chapter but a

64

fresh look at the structure and deployment of the workforce may help in these circumstances. Managers must try to forecast the demand for each type of employee, and identify which can be shifted from low-demand to high-demand assignments when needed.

Organizations could also be accused of exploiting their support staff by not paying them a proper rate for the job. Library assistants can see the increase in their duties as increased pressure rather than increased interest. They may resent having to do more work for the same wage and begrudge taking on 'professional' duties without any corresponding increase in status or pay. Library assistants believe that they regularly undertake tasks which ought really to be handled by qualified librarians and although they often see this as an essential part of their job satisfaction, there is a danger that they could suffer from role overload as they attempt to cope with tasks and duties for which they have not received adequate training. The increase in assistants' duties and responsibilities has often been haphazard with no structure and with little discussion of benefits or drawbacks. Managers should make a concerted effort to clarify new roles and responsibilities, and a job profile specially tailored to the unit's requirements and staff member's own skills, experience and developmental needs is vital.

A brief look at any advertisement for library vacancies is enough to convince anyone of the need for staff at all levels to be 'flexible' and 'adaptable' and a job description in the classic sense may be viewed as limiting managers' ability to change the nature of support staff work as and when needed. Uncertainty and change can force changes in roles and organization structure which make job descriptions rapidly obsolete. Moreover, they can be viewed as restricting the development of teams of flexible multi-skilled workers with each person performing a range of operations. This functional flexibility has led to reduced demarcation between jobs and arguably greater efficiency, but support staff were rarely contracted to take on the extra duties, responsibilities and accountabilities they are now handling when they were first recruited.

Although job descriptions or profiles can be viewed as prescriptive and not supporting market drives and changes (Raddon, 1991), research has shown that employees who feel they have accurate job descriptions are more satisfied with the organization, believe the employer is trustworthy and supports its workers, and express a lower desire to change jobs (Taylor, 1994). Although there are problems in describing and defining jobs with a complex skills mix, library employers could draw up developmentally oriented job descriptions to enable job holders to deal with uncertainty. Instead of using job descriptions solely to communicate management objectives to employees, library organizations could use them to clarify job tasks between supervisors and their support staff; identify conditions that make performance of specific tasks easy or difficult; and set objectives and performance criteria for individuals. Constructed along these lines, job descriptions can increase the clarity of job-related communication between support staff and their line managers (Klingner, 1979).

The smooth introduction of any innovation, be it a new service or a new way of providing an existing one, will be facilitated by ensuring each job holder has clear expectations and the necessary information and support to enable him or her to cope with the developments. Management has a responsibility to clarify how various employee roles have changed as a result of reorganization.

Physical working conditions

Managers also have an obligation to provide a safe and healthy working environment for their employees. Although there is a tendency to play down the importance of physical working conditions, a good working environment can raise production and morale (Isacco, 1985). A monetary value cannot easily be placed on improvements in the working environment. Seeking better working conditions for staff is not a matter of 'feather-bedding' staff. There is a clear relationship in the minds of staff and managers between working conditions and stress, the ability to respond to pressures, staff turnover and the quality of work (Hayes et al., 1989). Unfortunately, libraries are often reported as being overcrowded, lacking in privacy, cluttered and noisy which means that library staff:

> ...are often forced to perform their duties in environments that have a deleterious influence on their professional and personal lives (Bold, 1982, p. 1050).

Staff interviewed for the research reported here, however, had often not noticed a marked deterioration in their physical working conditions, and some were more satisfied in new or newly refurbished libraries. This is not to deny that problems exist in some areas. Lack of ready cash means that broken equipment may not be immediately replaced and there is inadequate provision for the decoration, maintenance and repair of premises:

> I think we're beginning to see the effect of diminishing resources on the fabric of our buildings. Part of that is the dwindling economic climate, part of that is pigeons coming home to roost - perhaps the preventive work's not been done in the past. I am conscious of the number of buildings that our staff work in which are not as I would like them to be. I think they should be better

66

and I know that we don't have the resources either to improve them or replace them (senior manager, metropolitan borough).[3]

Tougher legislation concerning health and safety at work has meant that there have been improvements, and management is probably more aware of these kinds of issues. Services may find staff taking action to force improvements in their working environment as service point staff, too, are increasingly better informed about their rights in this area, and often make it quite clear that they are not prepared to put up with sub-standard working conditions.

Many public libraries, in particular, date from the turn of the century and are suffering the ravages of time apart from anything else. This problem of an ageing building stock is aggravated by a lack of maintenance as repairs budgets are stagnating and even declining in real terms. The time it often takes for faults or repairs to be attended to, and the lack of general maintenance work like decorating are other concerns. However, while front-line staff are perturbed about the condition of their buildings and stock, and the impact of any inadequacies on their users, senior management are generally more preoccupied with balancing the budget and making ends meet just to keep services running. Although managers are also concerned with the condition of the buildings and employees' work environment, many other more pressing problems demand their immediate attention.

Another aspect of physical working conditions touched on above is workload. An increasing workload can take its toll on library assistants' physical well-being. Less staff, especially library assistants, means more counter work and shelving duties for everybody. Under-staffing can mean that staff spend far longer on their feet and do more 'running about', leading to fatigue. The rate at which tasks have to be carried out, as well as the lack of opportunity to do anything else, can be mentally as well as physically draining.

New ways of working can have an effect on the physical health of staff in other ways too. The introduction of information technology into libraries, for example, may cause a deterioration in the quality of library assistants' physical working environment:

Chronic eye fatigue is epidemic among library workers as are backaches, cramps and a general malaise born of chronic tedium and exhaustion (Kelly, 1990, p 15).

Managers must pay sufficient attention to the physical side of automation and change generally if they want to avoid morale problems. Creating and maintaining a quality work environment presents a wide variety of challenges

67

and considerations for management. The concerns of the people operating in the work space must be considered at least as much as the impression presented to users. The attention given to fixtures and fittings can say a lot about how much the organization values its staff and is concerned about their health and welfare. Care taken to establish a pleasant work environment is a sound investment. Providing a comfortable space for staff to relax and meet informally is also important. The one-off costs of improvements can be substantially less that the health care costs resulting from poorly designed work areas, and the potentially adverse effects on employees' physical and psychological health of a shoddy working environment.

Conditions of work

Establishing a satisfactory working climate also means considering what individual workers hope to receive from work. A successful manager will find out what subordinates' needs are and will attempt to arrange work to satisfy some of these needs. Maslow's hierarchy of needs (Maslow, 1943) is still a useful guide to what compels individuals to work and try to achieve in the workplace, although how much this is under managerial control has been questioned (Evans, 1992). Nevertheless, the desire for safety, including a steady job and income, and the desire for esteem in the form of status are important facets of working life for most employees.

Job security

Gruneberg (1979) asserts that job security is a classic example of one of Herzberg's hygiene factors, all-consuming when absent, leading to unhappiness and dissatisfaction but apparently unimportant when the individual's job is not under threat. Thus, job security is "more fundamental to job satisfaction than any other aspect of the job" (Gruneberg, 1979, p. 63) because the major dichotomy in our society is between those with a job and those without.

Commentators insist that 'a job for life' is a relic of a dim and distant past as employment security becomes less and less obtainable (Lee, 1994). Employees in the public sector are experiencing this just as much as those in the traditionally less secure private sector. Indeed,

> ...the image of the public sector as a protected bastion of secure jobs and programs has been dramatically eroded. Such expectations have become permanently violated (Jick, 1985, p. 84).

News of job freezes and budgetary constraints unsurprisingly provoke anxiety about security among employees which can be very damaging to motivation and morale. Insecurity can lead to feelings of helplessness and resistance (Hannon, 1982), and the level of job satisfaction an employee experiences will decline with the increasing intensity of 'job anxiety', defined as:

> ...the apprehension, fearful and pessimistic feelings or imagination of the employees about themselves and about various aspects of his job (Prasad and Singh, 1989, p.159).

Most library services have reduced their establishments by freezing vacant posts rather than through redundancy programmes although, generally, staff probably feel less secure now for a number of reasons. One of these is the tendency to employ more people on temporary contracts as library and information work is increasingly financed on a short term basis and takes the form of projects that have a limited life span. Unsure about their future staffing budget, employers are wary of committing themselves to permanent contracts. Other library services have increased the number of part-time assistants they employ.

The benefits and drawbacks of these flexible workforce strategies for both library employer and employee will be discussed in greater detail in chapter 6 but at this point it is important to note that one of the disadvantages for the employee is a decline in job security. Even part-timers on permanent contracts can still fear that their jobs will be the first to be lost if cuts have to be made:

> [I don't feel] very secure because of all this upheaval, recession. They tell us, 'Oh you'll be redeployed' but you still think, especially being a part-timer, you think they can just tell you at a week's notice 'Oh, your job is to go'. They do reassure us but I think I'm still not secure, even having worked here for five or six years (library assistant, metropolitan borough).[4]

Individual's personal circumstances can also effect how secure they feel at any one time. Those who feel they have more to lose if they are made redundant place greater emphasis on job security. These staff may experience a heightened pressure to perform as they feel they have to make an extra effort just to prove how capable and indispensable they are. In this situation, fear of job loss can replace more traditional incentive schemes, but this is hardly likely to inspire much creativity or enthusiasm (Rubin, 1984).

The restructuring process can thus be very unsettling with rumours of job losses and redeployment rife. Management should make a special effort to communicate in these circumstances and allay the fears of staff. When times are hard, any evidence of change can be interpreted as instability raising fears about job security (Harvey and Spyers-Duran, 1984). The internal restructuring that many library services have been, and are, undertaking has led many staff to fear for their positions and the content of their jobs.

In the public sector, restructuring at a higher level, national or local government level, can also provoke insecurity. Changes to local government finance, education reforms and local government reorganization have left many fearing the next government proclamation:

> I would say, at the moment, there is an aura of insecurity over everybody in local government and I would suspect that if perhaps you're at the lowest strata, again, you probably feel vulnerable and lost (senior manager, county council).[5]

In the study reported here, although there were staff members who, for various reasons, were feeling less sure of their positions than they once did, the majority of support staff members still seemed to feel relatively secure in their jobs. Thirty-nine support staff respondents (59%) answered that they felt secure in their jobs. Often they added a qualifier such as 'fairly', 'pretty' or 'reasonably' and sometimes suffixed this with 'at the moment' or 'in the short term', but their replies still indicated that the majority of assistants were not worried about the immediate security of their jobs.

Individual members of the support staff can carve out quite a niche for themselves and feel totally secure. Staff can also view restructuring not as something to be feared, but more as an opportunity to be grasped:

> [I feel] fairly secure. I'm interested to see what's happening in the future, there's obviously something around the corner. I'd like to be aware sort of exactly what it's going to mean but at present, yes, fairly secure (paraprofessional, county council).[6]

Much appears to hinge on issues of authority and control. Those paraprofessionals higher up the support staff and organizational hierarchy often feel able to direct their own future to a large extent and certainly more than others of the support staff who feel they have little influence over the direction their job will take. Differences in managerial style may explain why some support staff feel they have a greater degree of authority over their work life than others, and confidence in management is also a crucial factor.

70

Uncertain themselves about likely outcomes, management may often find it difficult to reassure staff, leading to a lack of confidence about the future.

Reorganizations are a major initiative and take a considerable time to complete, prolonging the period of uncertainty, and, in the process, there is a danger of relations between managers and staff becoming poisoned. Managers should make an effort to empower their support staff and so reduce the feeling of helplessness that can become debilitating in the face of restructuring. Services undergoing major changes could consider setting up a task force to investigate all the issues surrounding reorganization. Involving all levels of staff, such initiatives can help channel staff energies in a positive way and encourage their contribution, so preventing them feeling distant from the process and in the dark as to what is going on.

In the past, hard work, expertise and knowledge earned job security. Loyalty was the essence of the relationship between employer and employee. Employers promised job security and a steady progression up the hierarchy in return for the employee's commitment. However, there is growing agreement that this standard concept of job security is dead (Waterman et al, 1994). The challenge, though, is not to replace the traditional concept of job security with something closely resembling it, but rather to move towards a more collaborative relationship between employer and employee. With management help, employees can learn to manage their anxieties about job security and the direction of their careers as they adapt to the new ways of working brought about by restructuring. Communication is the key. Employers must provide an honest and realistic assessment of short and long term prospects for the organization.

Library and information organizations today may not be able to guarantee lifetime job security but they should instead offer workers meaningful work, experience and the opportunity to develop the skills and flexibility necessary to respond to changing market requirements. Assertive individuals with well-defined career goals, based upon personal skill and experience, will be at a distinct advantage in the new workplace environment. Managers can help individuals develop this pro-active attitude by instilling in their workers self-confidence, a sense of personal responsibility, and tolerance for ambiguity. Working with the employee, the employer can enhance the individual's usefulness within the service, and employability outside the organization, by encouraging staff to grow, change and become more self-reliant. A clear statement of management expectations can be a powerful reassurance to employees at the mercy of an uncertain environment.

While they may no longer have complete job security, individuals will have a job with the organization as long as they 'add value' to its operations. In return, staff have the right to demand interesting and important work, the freedom and resources to perform it well, and the experience and training

71

needed to be employable in that service or elsewhere (Reilly, 1994). A new psychological contract between library services and their staff needs to be established, one that offers something instead of job security in return for employees' commitment and performance. The employer must invest in its workers, providing work that stretches the individual's capabilities, and ensuring that the job adds value to both the individual and the organization while sharing information about what is happening to the service.

Promotion

Instead of job security, then, the organization should offer employees the opportunity to improve or acquire skills and enhance their experience. This can lead to frustration, however, if development is not rewarded or formalised by advancement up the organizational hierarchy. For library support staff, restructuring and organizational change is rarely accompanied by corresponding radical adjustments to promotion systems. Formal and informal changes in roles have encouraged support staff to think of themselves as capable of more complicated tasks, and they are beginning to behave in ways that reflect this by asking for opportunities to increase their responsibilities and, in the process, move up the organizational hierarchy.

In the past, it may have been assumed that library support staff were 'birds of passage' (Igbafe, 1984) who viewed library employment as a job not a career (Fitch, 1990). Other studies, however, have found library support staff as concerned as professional librarians about status and growth (e.g. Clemens, 1983, Gill, 1981) and this is supported by evidence gathered for the research on which this book is based. The managers interviewed generally agreed that support staff display considerable commitment and dedication to their work, and interviews with support staff reinforced the argument that library assistants attach as much importance as professionals to recognition and achievement, and need a clear vision of their future prospects to maintain their morale and motivation. Although individuals can gain a great deal of their job satisfaction from intrinsic elements of their work such as autonomy, responsibility and the feeling of having done a job well, the importance of extrinsic motivation factors like payment, career structures and promotion prospects should not be overlooked (Core, 1991).

The Library Association's decision to allow paraprofessionals and library assistants to join the L.A. as Affiliated Members can be interpreted as long-overdue recognition of the value of paraprofessionals and their commitment to their work. However, these 'career' assistants are feeling increasingly frustrated by a system which will not acknowledge them (Taylor, 1981) and the L.A. decision is at least one attempt to compensate for the lack of recognition, and to encourage paraprofessional involvement and sense of commitment.

Nevertheless, career development is probably the single issue which causes most resentment among library assistants (Castelyn, 1991). It was over twenty years ago that Lester Asheim (1967) wrote of the desirability of the establishment of a career for support staff. Even earlier than that Muller (1965) was advocating a support staff classification and pay plan which would provide a sufficient number of classes to allow for differences in the complexity of work.

Today, low turnover, frozen posts and declining establishments, the result of budgetary constraints, exacerbate the difficulties faced by library assistants eager to take on more responsibility and progress up the career ladder although some institutions have adapted their staffing structures to allow for paraprofessional promotion. University libraries offer the position of senior library assistant to experienced support staff while, as mentioned earlier, team librarianship in public libraries has resulted in many assistants being promoted to supervisory grades (Russell, 1986). In 1979, when the concept of team librarianship was still quite new, it was hoped that the transfer of day-to-day responsibility for service points from professionals to support staff would be the vehicle for an improvement in the job content, and hopefully the pay, for library assistants (Moore, 1979). Today, support staff can work their way up to become library managers often earning considerably more than young professionals.

The restructuring of library service staffing patterns has, thus, often improved career opportunities for library assistants. In some services this means that many support staff can advance to the same level as beginning librarians and even higher:

> For years, if you were a library assistant, you were on scale 1, if you were lucky in a large library you could possibly get on to a scale 2 as a senior library assistant whereas now most people are in fact on scale 2, apart from new members of staff, and they at least do have the promotion prospects of assistant branch manager and if they're really ambitious of branch manager. Branch managers in a large branch are actually on scale 5 now so the promotion aspects I think are there (librarian, London borough).[7]

Giving support staff the opportunity to run what are quite large service areas in some cases, is a great change for the better and gives assistants something to aim for. In public libraries, it is in the branches that the promotion opportunities offered by the introduction of new staffing structures have undergone the most radical change. Professional staff have often been removed from branch libraries giving support staff the chance to advance up the branch hierarchy. New posts like branch manager or supervisor have been created, opening more senior positions for assistants.

73

Thus, assistants have often benefited from the alterations to staffing patterns made necessary by changing economic circumstances and the need to respond positively to them:

> Because of the economic climate there have been, necessarily, redundancies, early severance, things like that, reorganizations. Very often the opportunities for those who remain after that kind of exercise are better, it actually creates opportunities (senior manager, metropolitan borough).[8]

Under pressure many library services have had to examine their staffing policies and as a result have created new posts for support staff, often of an administrative nature, which gives assistants something to aim for as well as recognition, improved status and a more promising career structure. It should be remembered, however, that in the present economic climate, any structural changes to enhance career prospects may well be abandoned, or at least limited, as organizations find it difficult to meet wage rises accompanying up grading.

Career paths for all grades of staff have become increasingly restricted (John Fielden Consultancy, 1993) but in times of economic stringency the few opportunities for advancement at support staff level become even scarcer. Attempts to enhance prospects by attending library school or even higher education college are also severely hampered as services are reluctant to release the staff member and the necessary finance, and are unable to guarantee that there will be a permanent post available for the newly qualified.

As table 4.1 indicates, a substantial majority of support staff disagree to some extent that their promotion prospects have improved. The fact that only 15% of both library assistant and paraprofessional respondents chose 'neither agree nor disagree' indicates that there are strong feelings on this issue.

Table 4.1
Responses to statement, 'My promotion prospects have improved over the last five years/since I started work here'

	paraprofessionals	library assistants
strongly agree	5%	0%
agree	10%	15%
neither agree nor disagree	15%	15%
disagree	65%	48%
strongly disagree	5%	22%

The 'flat pyramid' personnel structure common in library services, with large numbers of staff employed at service point level, means that opportunities to advance are scarce. Limitations on mobility and chances of advancement are leaving lower level staff feeling trapped and staff are becoming over-qualified and frustrated in the positions they occupy. The grading level of posts *should* be determined by reference to the duties and responsibilities being carried out (Library Work, 1989), but in libraries, one of the major problems appears to be that positions and not people are graded. This locks individuals into low level job classifications and even if they learn new skills and perform at significantly higher levels than previously, they cannot advance unless their positions are reclassified (McCann et al., 1990). However much extra responsibility staff take on, once they reach the top of the support staff grading system there is no further they can go.

A lack of career prospects is often the most dissatisfying aspect of work for library support staff and, increasingly, staff believe that the lack of professional qualifications should not prevent them advancing to more senior managerial positions. Fiercely committed to their library services and keen to put developmental ideas into practice, paraprofessionals, in particular, are often frustrated at their inability to advance. These staff often do not want to take a professional degree, believing they should be able to move up the management hierarchy, perhaps to area management level, without qualifications in librarianship. With teams of professional librarians below her/him, the area manager would just be in a supervisory position, administering and overseeing the team.

The obvious rejoinder would be that if, as a library assistant, an individual can advance to the same level as a librarian, what is the point of going to library school? The in-depth study and understanding of library work and its environment that a library school education provides, enabling practitioners to take an overview of services and carry them forward, is indispensable as is the support of the body of national professional opinion which professionally qualified staff have at their disposal and which they can use to represent and, if necessary, defend library services within their authority.

Others argue quite persuasively that there is no reason to dictate that career progression in the library service should only be in terms of the accumulation of experience and/or competence in library or information handling skills. As the NALGO's 'Guidelines for Action' (1989) suggest:

> There is, in fact, a wide range of managerial skills, supervisory and other organizational skills which can and should be developed and properly recognised. In other local government services there is a wide variety of administrative, financial, personnel and similar functions which are open to suitably

qualified people who may not be qualified in the primary function of that particular department. This obviously leads to considerable career opportunities running across departments. It is often difficult for library assistants to make progress towards more senior levels of administrative, financial or personnel functions unless they become qualified in librarianship (NALGO, 1989, p. 7).

Similarly, in a pamphlet entitled 'Who Manages the Library?', Val Wallace (1992) investigates the position of paraprofessionals and describes the kind of organizational structures and training which will allow them to rise to senior managerial posts. She stresses that the skills of the professionally qualified staff need not be diluted or challenged in any way because of the separation of managerial and library skills.

The professional 'bar' to promotion seems likely to continue anyway for the near future and as long as it does there should at least be opportunities and encouragement for assistants to gain professional qualifications or pursue courses which will help them improve their status. Another simple solution may be to introduce an appraisal scheme which pays attention to the amount of training assistants undertake and the responsibility they take on. The more they do, the more likely they are to be given an upgrading which seems a logical move towards a progressive career structure that rewards individuals and the skills and experience they bring to their posts rather than fixing rigid grades to particular jobs. A sensible and coherent personnel structure which confers on paraprofessionals a distinct role and place in the organization will not only acknowledge the unique contribution they make to the library, but will also give young library assistants something to aim for and a rational career progression.

Paraprofessionals are now moving into positions which increasingly involve managerial responsibilities. A separate support staff career ladder which acknowledges and formalises this will demonstrate management's commitment to developing its support staff. A new career structure with more opportunities should be accompanied by an appropriate reward system and a planned programme of training opportunities and targets. To rise up the support staff hierarchy, individuals should undertake a systematic training course leading to a qualification, such as the various levels of S/NVQ.

One of the principal obstacles encountered by any assistant eager to advance up the paraprofessional career ladder is the lack of more senior posts. It often seems to be a case of waiting to step into dead women's shoes as more and more increasingly well qualified and experienced people chase fewer jobs at senior supervisory level. Declining staff numbers has led to a decrease or, at the very least, a stagnation in the number of vacancies:

After so many years' experience , you might be encouraged to go for the senior library assistant [post], but they're cutting down and some of the smaller branches now only have one senior library assistant so there's just nowhere else to go, and if they're closing libraries then the SLA [senior library assistant] goes as well (librarian, metropolitan borough).[9]

Flatter organizations mean increased competition for higher level positions, and combined with slow, or non-existent growth, there is a danger of library support staff feeling they are in a dead-end job with few chances to advance. This appears to be one of the great problems facing managers whose library organizations are possibly in danger of losing very good people to other fields where they can exploit the administrative, inter-personal and management skills acquired in libraries, earn more money and enjoy better career prospects.

Library administrators protest that their organizations cannot afford to upgrade all support staff positions but perhaps they should be asking themselves whether they can afford *not* to make some attempt to improve the lot of their support staff because if measures are not taken, there is danger that more and more support staff will take the initiative and move away from library work. Not only do many paraprofessionals grow within their jobs and expand their personal abilities, but they also increase their employment potential as regards other outside organizations as they acquire valuable skills including familiarity with automated systems, word processing packages, record keeping, and dealing with orders and suppliers. It has been pointed out that,

...there are still no acknowledged national career paths or national career structures for library and information assistants and other professions are beginning to offer more lucrative openings to this technical level of staff. Our traditional library and information assistant markets have already become pools in which other professions are beginning to fish (Castelyn, 1991, p. 38).

A progressive career ladder is crucial to encourage good people to stay with the organization and make a career out of library support work. (Clemens, 1983). Good opportunities for advancement can enhance morale, motivation and, ultimately, productivity. To ensure the continued health of the organization, good employees must be retained and this can be achieved by, among other things, offering them recognition and career planning. One of the major problems organizations have to solve, therefore, is how to reward valuable people for remaining in the organization through difficult times (Levine, 1979).

77

A lack of growth, however, means that there are limited promotions and rewards available to motivate and retain successful and loyal workers. Employees may feel betrayed and confused. Upward mobility is part of the psychological exchange between employer and employee in which hard work and commitment lead to successive levels in the organizational hierarchy (Buch and Aldridge, 1990).

Because people traditionally view advancement as the most important indicator of success at work, lack of progress can come as an enormous shock with negative repercussions on job satisfaction, motivation and performance (Appelbaum and Finestone, 1994). The management of library services needs to address this problem and find a way of maintaining morale and commitment in a situation of declining internal promotion opportunities.

Managers may initially try to convince their staff that lack of promotion does not necessarily mean the end of the individual's growth and career development, and encourage staff to continue in a developmental frame of mind. A stable state need not necessarily entail stagnation. People who have reached the limit of their possible progress in the organization can still maintain growth and development as they acquire and use new skills, abilities and attitudes (Appelbaum and Finestone, 1994).

Managers have to help their 'plateaued' support staff come to terms with the fact that promotion opportunities are not guaranteed, but how this message is communicated to employees in this situation can either positively or negatively affect their performance (Carnazza et al, 1981). Individuals should be made to feel indispensable in their present posts and be assured that their performance is not to blame for their lack of progression. A period of stability can help employees consolidate their skills and experience and help them focus on the job they are doing and on ways that job, and their performance of it, can be improved. However, managers also have to consider the situation from the employee's point of view. For some individuals it might not be enough to hear how well they are doing their job, how much they are appreciated, and how valuable they are to the organization. In these cases ambition can become an organizational liability as lack of progression yields extreme frustration, low work involvement, dissatisfaction and poor performance (Bardwick, 1988).

As the economic prospect for libraries in all sectors is not particularly rosy, employees will have to come to terms with the fact that low growth for organizations, and slow progress for individuals within those organizations, will be a familiar feature of the employment scene in the late 1990s. Management has to find a way of convincing staff that career success can be achieved through increased responsibility rather than internal promotions.

Appointing support staff to task forces or working parties, and offering them interesting and meaningful work was suggested above as an alternative to conventional job security. Similar strategies could be employed to compensate for declining promotion opportunities. Individuals doing the same tasks at the same level for years do not only become frustrated at their lack of opportunity to progress to higher level work, but can also become bored with the routine. A lateral move, even temporarily, to a more 'interesting' job can be seen as a reward for good service where the long-standing employee's experiences and skill can be put to good use. Management must also try to conceive creative ways to enhance the responsibility and reward of present jobs. An experienced individual could be asked to develop and/or run training courses for new staff, or mentor younger employees.

As noted in chapter 1, project work can be immensely satisfying for support staff, giving individuals the opportunity to follow a piece of work through from conception to final product. Including them in task forces or working parties which can benefit from their experience can also help them stay productive and satisfied with their present position. Intrinsic job rewards and recognition can thus be crucial in mitigating the effects of career stagnation (Hall, 1985).

The management of library services need to equip their support staff with the skills and attitudes that will help them adjust to the change in the ways careers are conceived. Even large organizations cannot guarantee steady progress up the hierarchy for good employees. Career planning can help individuals plan their development by identifying the skills needed by their present employer, and even the next.

However, although analysts proclaim an end to job security and promotion opportunities, it seems likely that the reward system in libraries will continue to be the subject that raises the most heated comments from support staff, particularly the issue of pay.

Pay

> Oh, just don't get them [support staff] started on pay. They're
> all convinced that they're dreadfully underpaid, all of them, every
> last one of them (librarian, county council).[10]

There is still disagreement about the motivating power of a money. It is often argued that wage rises increase satisfaction just in the short term and that pay is only really important when it is considered to be unfair or is below subsistence levels (Hannabuss, 1983). Wage levels often have more significance than their buying power because salary is intimately related to status and can be seen as a measure of success, value or the respect in which the individual is held by others. When an employee's wage, and therefore rank, is lower than s/he feels is deserved, the individual feels unappreciated and to some degree dissatisfied.

Library assistants and their line managers often feel very strongly that support staff are underpaid and undervalued, and believe that for the amount of responsibility library assistants are given these days, the pay is really quite poor. This is also true of paraprofessionals. Although the more progressive grading structures introduced into many libraries have allowed support staff to advance up the career ladder and earn as much as professional librarians in some cases, staff at this paraprofessional level still frequently feel underpaid and believe that the considerable increase in responsibility and duties in their posts should be appropriately rewarded:

> I'm on scale 6 which is what most basic librarians are on, but in terms of the actual duties I have I feel that I could probably be higher. I think a fair grade would be something like SO1 because apart from the staffing responsibilities, I have a lot of financial responsibilities, I do most of the budget work on salaries and other types of things (paraprofessional, London borough).[11]

Senior managers often agree that much more is demanded of assistants now, and feel that they deserve material recognition of this. They acknowledge that library assistants and paraprofessionals are not paid enough and that their expectations of this section of staff far exceed what would probably be expected of someone in retail or the private sector paid a comparative wage. However, they also take the pragmatic view that the money to improve the situation is not readily available. The number of staff that would be involved makes it unlikely that radical or large scale rises will be given. Thus, even when management accepts that something needs to be done to improve the grading and pay structure of library support staff, financial circumstances often makes action impossible.

In many organizations, adequate compensation is inhibited by inappropriate salary correlations that continue to be made at a higher level between increasingly complex paraprofessional positions and totally unrelated jobs in retail and business offices. These traditional analogies are no longer useful, and can severely depress paraprofessional salaries and status (Oberg, 1992). Senior library managers should make a greater effort to make administrators and personnel officers aware of the magnitude of changes in the job descriptions of library support staff, and convince them that comparisons with the retail sector are no longer valid.

Commentators in the library and information world seem to fear that support staff will compare their wages with those of their professionally qualified colleagues, leading to conflict and division between the grades (e.g.

Billings and Kern, 1990; Russell, 1985). In the study reported here, there was little evidence of this, however. Assistants, librarians and senior officers do believe that support staff ought to be rewarded for the extra, 'professional' duties they now undertake, but this feeling of being undervalued on the part of assistants does not appear to translate itself into hostility towards their better paid professional colleagues, rather in a sense of grievance towards higher management. Library assistants and paraprofessionals *do* compare themselves with others but with workers outside libraries, and in public libraries, most often with other local authority workers. Unfortunately, library support staff find their own pay often compares very unfavourably and they are becoming increasingly discontent, often directing their dissatisfaction and frustration at library management.

Generally, support staff attitudes towards pay could be said to provide evidence which supports Lawler's discrepancy theory (Lawler, 1971). Lawler argued that pay satisfaction is viewed as a function of the perceived discrepency between (1) the amount of money a person feels they should receive on the job, and (2) the amount of money they actually receive. The standard against which a person compares his or her pay is a judgement of what s/he thinks the job should pay. This judgement is not influenced by what a person would like to receive but rather primarily by the following equity factors: perceived personal job inputs; perceived inputs and outcomes of referent others; perceived job characteristics; perceived non-monetary outcomes and wage history.

Library assistants compare what their work requires from them in terms of skill, experience, effort, and present and past performance with that of other council workers (in public libraries), or workers in retail or office-based jobs, and what *they* are paid. Library support staff contrast the responsibility, task difficulty, dedication, hours worked and public contact involved in their work with that of these 'referent others' and are often dissatisfied with their pay in comparison.

Considering the disparity between what library assistants are now expected to do and the wage they are paid, *and* considering that they are generally aware of this discrepancy, it is surprising that more library services have not been confronted with regrading claims from library support staff. Only a handful of articles dealing with equity campaigns have appeared in the library literature, however (Kirkland, 1991). The root of the problem may lie in the fact that library work at all levels is 'a feminine profession' and that a woman's expectations of her salary are lower that those of a man. Norms of social resignation and compliance with authority in traditional female occupations may be to blame for the absence of protest over pay (Steel and Lovrich, 1987). It could thus be argued that paraprofessionals suffer by working within a female-dominated profession and from the effects of female socialisation into passive roles (Oberg et al, 1991). This and other aspects of equal opportunities will be examined in greater detail in chapter 6.

External economic conditions can also have an effect on satisfaction with wages and the action staff can take to improve their position:

> I think [assistants] are aware, some of the younger ones, that they have skills and if they were to be positive they could probably get a better paid job, but the economic climate is changing all the time. Not so long ago they could have done that, I think now it would be less easy to do it. They're probably glad to have a job (librarian, county council).[12]

Knowing there is little chance of a quick and successful outcome in today's service environment, few seem willing to take a stand against low pay, inequitable career structures, recruitment freezes and cutbacks.

Support staff complaints about their wages, however, are often balanced by other aspects of their work that they feel make up for their poor remuneration. For some it is the convenience of their library while for others it is the job satisfaction their work affords them. Parallels can be drawn with other service professionals such as nurses who are similarly highly motivated to do their jobs but have been neglected in terms of proper remuneration for what they do.

Library managers must not take advantage of this, however, nor of the fact that there is rarely a problem in filling support staff positions from the large pool of willing applicants that generally exists. A high turnover is inefficient and expensive and managers should be keen to retain experienced staff, as well as fulfil their responsibility to pay their support staff what they think they are worth. The aim should always be to pay people for their contribution to organizational objectives, and the basis for an effective compensation scheme is a clear view of the value of individual positions.

Each position has a relative 'job size' that corresponds to its importance in achieving service objectives (Sahl, 1994). This puts the emphasis on the work carried out rather than an individual's place in the organizational hierarchy. Library support staff should be assigned a value that represents their contribution to organizational goals. The increasing range of skills and responsibilities library assistants and paraprofessionals have acquired need to be recognised and formalised in a more equitable pay structure. Apart from anything else, it is a concrete sign that management appreciates their efforts and values their contribution to the library service.

> Sometimes, I feel that we do a good job and we don't get the appreciation that we deserve because a lot of people still tend to

82

think that libraries are just there for people to walk in, get a book and walk out again and there's a lot more to it than that (library assistant, metropolitan borough).[13]

Library managers need to grasp the twin nettles of pay and promotion to ensure that support staff do realise they are appreciated and to establish their value and importance to the organization, thus developing a fair and motivating working environment for their support staff.

Working relations

A crucial factor in establishing this happy and productive working atmosphere for library support staff is the promotion of conditions conducive to positive working relations with both colleagues and users. The physical and social environment of work can have a significant effect on worker morale and satisfaction (Mehrabian, 1990), and the need for social interaction with others is one of the lower order described by Maslow (1943). This basic need for supportive relations at work could become even more important in times of organizational change or crisis. Talking about stress can help reduce burnout by establishing a feeling of 'esprit de corps' and reinforcing a sense of personal worth. Good relations at work can also compensate for the diminution of other extrinsic benefits or satisfying aspects of a job like upward mobility. As chapter 2 explained, constrained organizational circumstances can put pressure on this aspect of work, but there are actions managers can take to ensure that any disagreements do not become debilitating for the organization, and distressing for staff.

Support staff relations with professional librarians

Many writers in the LIS field do not perceive increasing co-operation as a result of restructuring and the gradual convergence of 'professional' and 'non-professional' tasks discussed in previous chapters (see e.g. Core 1991; Billings and Kern 1990). On the contrary, the fact that the two groups of employees share many duties but are regarded quite differently by employers has reportedly led to resentment being expressed by library assistants.

The perception that many paraprofessional and professional tasks overlap may provoke charges of unfair treatment and pay rates from support staff while professionally qualified staff feel frustrated. Moreover, a lack of information flowing between the grades, heightened during times of uncertainty, can also cause despondency. All these problems can result in a divided staff (Baker, 1986).

It has been suggested that librarians and paraprofessionals often misunderstand each other's role. While paraprofessionals appear not to comprehend the scope of the responsibilities that librarians bear and perceive themselves to be doing equivalent work, librarians may misconstrue the resentment that the support staff feel, patronise them and underestimate their commitment to the library and the service (Oberg, 1991).

It is probable that the gap between professionals and their support staff will continue to narrow as the economic climate forces pragmatic decisions based on the availability of resources. Thus, the definition of 'professional' and 'non-professional' work is constantly changing and, taken together, these trends can increase the potential of conflict between the two categories of staff.

Table 4.2

Responses to statement, 'The relationship between professional librarians and library assistants has improved over the last five years/since I started work here'

	paraprofessionals	library assistants
strongly agree	10%	6%
agree	45%	50%
neither agree or disagree	40%	22%
disagree	5%	22%
strongly disagree	0%	0%

In fact, as table 4.2 illustrates, the majority of respondents in the study reported here felt that the relationship between librarians and support staff had improved; the 'them and us' situation is not as prevalent now; co-operation has increased; and the demarcation lines between professional and support staff tasks are less defined.

Restructuring and change can thus have a beneficial effect on the relationship between professional librarians and support staff. The use of working groups or teams, taking staff from various grades to develop new services and policies, helps break down any barriers that might exist between different grades (John Fielden Consultancy, 1993). Assistants are now frequently in charge of individual service points with professional services arranged either centrally or on a team basis. One could cynically argue that this has improved relations as professionals and assistants rarely come into contact with one another and so the opportunity for conflict over procedures or practices is minimal. In these circumstances, professionals and support staff may encounter one another only on a social basis where there is less chance of status or position being conspicuous.

An emphasis on team-building can dissipate any resentment along with an effort to communicate to professional librarians that the widening of the paraprofessional role is not a threat and can only be to their benefit as it releases them to do work appropriate to their training. As paraprofessionals prove they can do a good job, and take much of the administrative burden of running service points from professional shoulders, so there should be more acceptance of their role. This is the ideal scenario, but in practical terms difficulties can be encountered.

Although this book has concentrated on outlining how support staff are increasingly taking on 'professional' duties, less attention has been paid to the other side of the coin, where professionally qualified librarians have to undertake clerical and routine duties normally carried out by their assistants:

> Professional staff are spending a lot more time doing routine work, issuing books, basically making sure that the service points are covered, the library stays open. So I think that will have changed the relationship to some degree because they're basically working together more (senior officer, metropolitan borough).[14]

Thus, working relationships can change because of staffing difficulties. Although it is desirable that staff are willing and able to take on extra duties outside their job descriptions in any emergencies that occur, they should not be expected to carry on doing them long term. Often, staffing levels are so tight that if assistants were not prepared to take on some professional duties and professionals some of the routine, house-keeping tasks from time to time, the library would grind to a halt. Despite the fact that this can result in a closer working relationship for many staff, this is an undesirable trend. Individuals should not have to do work inappropriate to their job descriptions for any length of time just to ensure the service keeps running and the libraries stay open. Apart from the fact that it is an uneconomic solution to the problem, it is also unwise and inefficient management suggesting a disregard of workforce planning.

Generally, however, a relaxation of the demarcation lines between professional and paraprofessional duties has come about as the result of the restructuring and deliberate redistribution of tasks and workload. Library managers need to put quite a bit of thought into how this flexibility can be achieved while preserving job satisfaction for all their staff and trying not to exploit any one section of it. A better mutual understanding of respective roles is needed and team work is the key with subject teams consisting of professional librarians and support staff who are trained and encouraged to participate and become more involved in the running of the library. This will increase communication between the grades which, in turn, will help improve the relationship in many cases.

This system ensures flexible, adaptable staffing patterns and encourages professionals and support staff to see themselves as part of the same team, dedicated to providing a high quality service. It also adds variety and interest to the jobs of the support staff. Whatever grade of staff an individual is, s/he should be encouraged to take an active part in the provision of the service, and this relies on a willingness to use individuals' expertise to develop and promote the library. A tendency to involve library assistants much more in areas of activity that were the traditional preserve of librarians and to seek their opinions on operational matters will demonstrate how much management values them. The recognition and credit library support staff receive in this way will undoubtedly have a beneficial effect on their morale:

> When I first started seven years ago I personally felt morale here was very low. As a library assistant you were the lowest of the low, whereas now there's a very different working atmosphere and you do feel that you are appreciated in what you do and I think it does make all the difference (paraprofessional, county council).[15]

Camaraderie can be bolstered by professional line managers acknowledging that their support staff have as important a role to play in the provision of the service as themselves. Above all, perhaps, professionals should be approachable, willing to help and available should any staff be having problems. A more relaxed social atmosphere is prevalent in libraries today anyway. Senior managers and librarians are usually known by their first names and are generally perceived as genial and accessible by support staff. This has been a gradual process over the last fifteen or twenty years and reflects changes in society at large:

> I think there is a general move away from an authoritative style of management to a more consultative and participative style of management which means bringing them [support staff] in. I mean, all my staff all call me by my first name. Now a few years ago I think that would have been a total impossibility with somebody in my position. Going back fifteen or twenty years that would have been the death knell to a library assistant, but I think that reflects changes in society, I don't think we're any different to industry in that sense and I think that's society rather than libraries particularly (senior manager, county council). [16]

Although societal changes can help, a greater willingness on the part of management at all levels to recognise the experience, skills and knowledge many assistants possess, to regard them as part of a team, and to try to involve them in as many aspects of the running of the library as possible will help overcome any resistance to changes in responsibility between professional and support staff. This policy will encourage staff to acknowledge each other as part of the same team working towards the same goals, and to accept the division of labour, tasks and roles.

Handled sensitively, both grades of staff will accomodate these trends. Although the blurring of tasks and roles may initially cause problems, as time goes on and staff adjust to their new positions a different type of co-operation and team work can emerge as individuals acknowledge that the various types and levels of work all have their validity and part to play in the overall provision of the service. Librarians have to be convinced that it is in their interest that paraprofessionals take over some of the administrative tasks they once had to undertake and be encouraged to recognise that support staff can sometimes perform these tasks more competently.

Thus, although it is generally accepted that economic and other changes can have an adverse effect on working relationships, it is less commonly acknowledged that they can also have the opposite outcome. In fact, communication between different sections and grades of staff can increase as the need to discuss difficulties is acknowledged, and co-operation and understanding between grades can strengthen as the need for everyone to pull together in any crisis that might arise is recognised. A similar closer working relationship can also be achieved among colleagues of the same level.

Relations among support staff

As chapter 1 illustrated, the results of the study reported here confirm those of previous studies which have found that co-workers are an important aspect of satisfaction with work for paraprofessional library staff, and it has been suggested that,

> The satisfactions in the job are social/human rather that task-related. They come from good interpersonal relations with others in the work group, and from dealing on a personal level with library customers (McKee, 1989, p. 119).

Restructuring and change, however, can lead to friction at work if competition, peevishness and concern about the future become overwhelming. In these circumstances managers need to strengthen and increase communications as the need to discuss difficulties is paramount. Co-operation and understanding need to be reinforced or perhaps restored to encourage staff to pull together in any crisis that might arise. Library assistants have always worked well together and managers may not have noticed a great change in relations among the support staff. There is generally a good working atmosphere in libraries and it is possible that this has improved over the years with everybody trying to do their best for their service.

The enlargement of assistants' roles and responsibilities offers managers scope for strengthening team work and co-operation. Giving support staff a specific role to play rather than regarding them just as 'juniors' helps in this respect. Reorganization which leaves paraprofessionals in charge of service points can also contribute. Giving support staff responsibility for certain functions means they need to co-operate more with their colleagues in other parts of the service, so encouraging staff to see themselves as part of a team and to work together. Although team work among support staff has always been very good, managers will find that interdependence makes for a very strong team and should actively strive to build a strong working unit which can cope with any crises or changes in policy that may arise.

A team approach among support staff can easily be encouraged because there is usually a larger group of them and they share a certain amount of work so they have to work more closely together as a group. Assigning assistants, as a group, their own projects can also facilitate this. The style of the individual library and manager can play a major role in the working atmosphere of the service point. Managers who rarely take much trouble over their support staff, hardly even knowing their names or anything about them, will not encourage commitment from staff. Feeling unappreciated, staff will be disinclined to put themselves out for others.

A supportive and interested supervisory climate, on the other hand, will encourage a co-operative atmosphere among support staff. If they feel valued and appreciated assistants will work well together and make a sterling effort to overcome any barriers to communication and collaboration that often exist in organizations undergoing change. Trust and openness are both vital in teamwork and the development of constructive working relationships. These inevitably lead to co-operation which means sharing resources, giving and receiving help, and dividing work. Trust is characterised by honesty, respect and the absence of defensive barriers so that staff can share information, thoughts, feelings and reactions to issues (Stott and Walker, 1995).

The recognition that staff are working together to provide a useful and needed service can enhance relations and conscious efforts at team-building, convincing everyone of the need to provide the best possible service despite any difficulties, will increase co-operation. Any divisions among staff are always worrying but even more so when all need to be united to respond positively to the changing environment. However, traditional constraints and structure become less important if all staff are encouraged to look for opportunities to improve the service.

The recruitment of individuals with good interpersonal skills, able to work well with their colleagues will help. The importance of recruitment procedures in ensuring that libraries engage support staff who can cope and maintain team spirit under pressure cannot be over-emphasised. An important consideration in any recruitment procedure is not just to match people with jobs, but also to ensure the individual will relate to the particular work group and its culture (McKee, 1989). The person specification has a very important role to play here by targeting people who have the social skills necessary for working well in a team environment. Making sure that new prospective support staff employees have the right interpersonal skills to deal with the public is also crucial.

Customer relations

The drive to make services more accountable to the people who use and pay for them should encourage library managers to examine and, if necessary, change their recruitment policies and practices. The importance of selecting 'people people' for library work is now generally recognised:

> We've made a number of decisions, particularly in staff selection, over the last few years which we've pursued quite aggressively. We choose people who get on with people, rather than people who are good at bibliographic work, to get away from the old library assistant syndrome - the bun, glasses and cardigan. We have a lot of very glamorous and very friendly ladies now (senior manager, county council).[17]

It is essential that library and information services recruit support staff who have the ability to relate sympathetically to members of the public without it being an effort. Although library-based skills are, of course, important, the first impression and responsiveness of the staff member are crucial for quality public relations.

For those already in post, positive customer care programmes reinforce the concept that being responsive and helpful aids relations, and can also increase job satisfaction in the process. As chapter 1 emphasised, library assistants often report that working with, or helping, the public was the aspect of their job they enjoyed the most, although it has also been noted that budgetary difficulties can result in a deterioration in user relations as staff have less time to spend with individuals. Despite difficulties like these that can arise, change and reorganization can mean that the relationship between library staff and library user improves. Extra training in customer care, for example, following restructuring or the introduction of new initiatives like the Library Charter or Total Quality Management, emphasises the importance of creating a welcoming, informal atmosphere for users.

Support staff have a crucial role to play here by being friendly and interested in user needs, and good interpersonal skills are vital if the library is to run a well-used and appreciated service. This also entails acting positively to complaints and comments about the service so that users leave the library feeling satisfied even if their information needs have not been met (Lund and Patterson, 1994).

Change and reorganization can improve customer relations in other ways too. The enlargement of the support staff role, for example, can also lead to better relations. As assistants' roles have expanded to include information work, so their job satisfaction has increased and so this has strengthened their relationship with the user. Giving paraprofessionals the freedom to run their own service points can makes an enormous different to their self-confidence which will help them in their dealings with users who possibly now have more respect for assistants:

> With the extra responsibility [support staff have] been given, I think to the enquirer, they're not just an assistant who will just fetch and carry for them but they are somebody with some knowledge of the subject who can help them (librarian, county council).[18]

In this way, support staff can forge a different sort of relationship with their users. Whereas previously a library assistant's job may have been very much clerical-based, concerned primarily with the issuing and discharging of materials, they are now becoming more involved in basic readers' advisory work and have much more direct contact with customers.

However, although quality initiatives, customer care programmes and the charter movement have made library organizations much more aware of their obligation to present an efficient and friendly face to customers, they have also made users much more aware of their rights. Services are now expected to be accountable, efficient and offer value for money. If the library falls short of any of these expectations, complaints will increase. As users become less tolerant of mistakes or inefficiency, so their attitude towards staff can suffer, and support staff are the staff members most likely to hear any criticisms·

The user demands more than we can provide, and therefore they get a little aggravated when we don't have it, and take it out on the assistants. They're, the front line and they're the ones who get the flak when things aren't as they want it (librarian, metropolitan borough).[19]

Cuts in services, or increases in charges and fines following budgetary restrictions can also encourage customer complaints. When user expectations are not met it is perhaps inevitable that users will become upset. Management should anticipate the repercussions on support staff/user relations before making decisions affecting the provision of service, and ensure that staff have the timely information and appropriate training to cope with any customer relations problems foreseen. This may include assertiveness training and other types of customer care skills which enables counter staff to deal in a courteous and confident manner with complainants instead of feeling powerless and a victim of the decision making process.

Violence and aggression from a range of people visiting libraries has become an increasing feature in recent years with growing concern about the problems of harassment, aggressive behaviour and violence encountered by staff. Libraries face a particular dilemma; they need and want to be welcoming and accessible, but their very openness means that staff are at risk from abusive behaviour from the public. However, staff should not be expected to work in an unsafe environment for the sake of maintaining a favourable public image. A recent survey (McGrath, 1995) found that a disturbingly high proportion of public library staff consider that verbal abuse is seen as part of the job. The incidence of this form of abuse was found to be very common and it seems that staff therefore regard it as inevitable and accept its occurrence.

Managers need to be aware of the difficult situations support staff on the front-line of the service often face. Public libraries, in particular, experience a wide range of problem users from irate customer to psychiatric patients in the community. Attacks can range from verbal abuse to sexual harassment and actual physical assault. Support from senior management is essential in these circumstances. Only when the problem is recognised can preventative measures be introduced. A first important step is an effective reporting system which must have the confidence of staff and be taken seriously by all parties. Proper evaluation of serious and less serious incidents will demonstrate to staff that managers are concerned for their safety and welfare, and it can also help pin-point when, why and how incidents occur so that preventative measures can be taken. Training is also important to help staff anticipate, diffuse and deal with incidents. Customer care training, assertiveness training and training to help staff handle aggression can equip front-line staff with the skills necessary to avoid confrontation, and, if necessary, techniques to deal with violence should it erupt (McGrath, 1995).

The previous paragraphs are not meant to suggest that support staff in libraries deserve danger money. However, managers do need to take these issues seriously. Various developments can lead to the relationship between the users and the staff becoming more impersonal and distant, and this possibly encourages less friendly relations. Information technology, for example, can make the library service appear detached and systematic and increasingly akin to a supermarket. Increasingly, workload and limited staffing numbers can similarly deprive the user and staff of much of the personal contact they once had, with little time to stop and chat. Nevertheless, services should still try to establish a friendly environment to which customers want to return, and in which staff want to work.

Conclusions

Library support staff have a right to a safe, comfortable, stable working environment which gives them the opportunity to use their skills and talents, and encourages them to develop as individuals and as members of the organization. Assistants are committed to providing users with a quality service but the working environment must be such that this is encouraged. Change, restructuring and budgetary crises can place a lot of stress on operational staff, especially if they feel they are not being rewarded in either monetary or status terms. The most dedicated staff in the world will find it difficult to work efficiently in conditions of tight staffing, with old and inadequate equipment, and with declining material resources. Although support staff often enjoy the actual content of their jobs, circumstances can make the performance of their duties difficult. Feeling that that they are not fulfilling their obligations to their users, staff can become disheartened and frustrated. The mental and physical challenge of constantly having to exert the maximum effort just to stand still may become too draining for some.

This trying situation will not encourage the development of confident, dynamic, purposeful information workers. On the contrary, the best workers may well become so frustrated and despondent in their positions that they 'vote with their feet'. An alternative scenario is the 'fight' syndrome whereby discontented staff fail to commit themselves or exert maximum effort to support the organization's goals (Vaughn and Dunn, 1974). The loss, or loss of interest, of these staff will be a tragedy as many of them have developmental ideas and are eager to take the service forward. Lack of progression, for themselves and their services, may make the brightest turn to others areas of employment where their talents and commitment can find more fertile ground.

Notes

1. Goulding, A. (1993), *Managing Public Library Support Staff in Times of Change*, p. 116
2. Ibid, p. 119
3. Ibid, p. 122
4. Ibid, p. 130
5. Ibid, p. 133
6. Ibid, p. 135
7. Ibid, p. 182
8. Ibid, p. 183
9. Ibid, p. 178
10. Ibid, p. 148
11. Ibid, p. 144
12. Ibid, p. 159
13. Ibid, p. 148
14. Ibid, p. 278
15. Ibid, p. 281
16. Ibid, p. 282
17. Ibid, p. 298
18. Ibid, p. 299
19. Ibid, p. 304

5 The organizational climate

Previous chapters have detailed how support staff in restructuring library organizations can experience feelings of anger, fear and guilt which can reduce productivity and undermine motivation and morale. Although changes to the way in which jobs are organized can add meaning to work and help people come to terms with change, to be successful in the long term the organization must reassess its operations, beliefs and values. Research indicates that 90% of change initiatives that fail do so because human factors were not taken adequately into account. Planning by senior managers must consider communication, employee involvement, support and training, and the organizational culture (Doe, 1994). The most critical factor leading to successful organizational change is the effective management of the human resource system. Employee involvement, communication and information sharing, appraising, training and articulating a vision are all critical aspects of successful reorganization (Cameron, 1994).

This chapter examines whether library managers have capitalised upon the forces for change, including the moves towards flatter structures, team working, and a more open management approach, examining in particular:

- management style, including information dissemination, consultation and participation;
- training and appraisal;
- organizational culture.

Management style

The need for management to sustain a healthy organization, whatever the external conditions, is crucial especially in times of change when organizational conditions liable to increase work stress are all the more likely (Tombaugh and White, 1990). An organizational climate in which an open, honest appraisal of important issues by all levels of staff is welcomed, can make a significant contribution to the adjustment of the workforce to change. Streamlining, reorganization and cutbacks, however, can erode employee trust and loyalty, presenting managers with opportunities and challenges related to employee communications (Clemons, 1994).

The information network

Information dissemination is the basis of a constructive dialogue between management and staff, and a lack of information about performance, instructions and decisions can promote the suspicion that superiors do not understand the problems that their support staff are facing. The inability to delegate or communicate can mean that instructions appear to emerge from an ivory tower, and are viewed as unworkable by the staff expected to provide a service for which they feel ill-equipped. Uncertain themselves about resources, management may find it difficult to reassure staff, but,

> Insufficient funding is not, however, an excuse for lack of communication, failure to include employees in decision making and a generally poor organizational climate. It may mean that management has to work that much harder to establish and maintain good working relationships with employees (Schneider, 1991, p. 400).

Faced with change employees have four basic common concerns:

- they want more information;
- they wonder how the change will affect them personally;
- they wonder what they need to do to implement the change;
- they wonder about the impact or benefit of the change (Blanchard, 1995).

Staff will, therefore, have numerous questions and managers must be prepared to explain how individuals will be affected; what they will be expected to do differently; how reporting relationships will change; how their performance will be evaluated; when the changes will be implemented; what the service will stop doing.

The successful management of change thus relies upon the frank and open exchange of information between staff and management. In libraries as in most other organizations, the most common formal communication channel between management and support staff is the meeting which takes place at various levels of the organization. In large library systems, information is cascaded through various levels of the hierarchy. In these circumstances,

95

senior support staff members have become important intermediaries between management and assistants, deciding how to report pieces of information, how important certain pieces of news are, and how they should be disclosed.

Although systems like these are in place, in practice they can fall down due to lack of time and pressure, and the need for confidentiality over certain subjects, especially financial matters. There is a danger of creating uncertainty and aggravating fear by sharing news of budget cuts, but suspicion is the child of ignorance and by informing employees of what is happening and how it will affect them, much resentment and anxiety can be avoided (Odini, 1990). Managerial silence certainly will not allay fears and might lead to what Levine (1984) terms the 'Tooth Fairy Syndrome'. Without a full and honest account of the situation, many staff may at first believe that decline is temporary and cuts will be restored - a possibility as remote as the Tooth Fairy.

The view that financial and policy decisions are irrelevant to support staff is outdated and generally untrue. Although details need not be given, support staff want to understand broad trends and are anxious to know the direction their services will be taking in the future:

> We're not really kept up to date. You might find out on the grapevine or you might find out because one or two members of staff will actually come forward and tell you things, but there are an awful lot of them at the top of the tree who think it's not for us to know. It *does* affect us and it *is* important (paraprofessional, metropolitan borough).[1]

There is a judgement to be made about how much staff need to know in order to make sense of their jobs, but managers should inform assistants of general trends and policies, and could do more to explain to them why and how decisions are reached. Information does need to be targeted to those individuals and teams who are able to interpret and act on it, but those higher up the organizational hierarchy should be increasingly willing to discuss such matters as budgets become tighter. There is often little they can do about the situation, and need to acknowledge that it is better that everyone in the organization knows the reality of the situation.

Staff need a realistic picture of the financial situation of the service and should be regularly updated and presented with the various alternatives proposed, or possible outcomes of negotiations. All library staff should have a basic understanding of the processes and decisions regarding the budget and future plans. At the very least this will enable them to give a knowledgeable response to library users enquiring, or complaining, about services. If staff understand the rationale behind decisions, they are also less likely to blame senior library management for problems with the service. Thus, managers should exclude nobody who could benefit from knowing pieces of information, but it is important that the data do not come in such volumes that individuals suffer from overload.

Although there are structures for passing on information, the problem of arranging meetings in a workforce with a great many part-time workers is an obstacle, as is the difficulty of finding time to get all staff together. In these circumstances, meetings can often fall by the wayside or become a mere formality. Increased pressure on senior management, too, can create a situation where important information reaches the professional ranks but is not always sent all the way down the line. Although it would be expected that those higher up the departmental hierarchy would be better, or more fully, informed, line managers, too, are not always fully in the picture which, of course, makes it very difficult for them to pass information on to their assistants:

> I don't think necessarily managers have got that information themselves. We tend to get bits and pieces of information from our own higher level of management, and I don't necessarily think it's being secretive, I think people find it very difficult, they don't know the whole situation themselves and they don't want to mislead or worry people (librarian, county council).[2]

Senior managers can have a paternalistic attitude as regards the imparting of information to their staff, deciding what is relevant or necessary for them to know. In a rapidly changing environment it is impossible to keep all staff completely up to date and managers, often unsure themselves about the latest developments, are probably wise to just sketch the broad outlines of policies and decisions and their implications for their staff. In spite of the 'communication chaos' that often prevails in the wake of restructuring, however (McGoon, 1994), managers must not neglect their duty to their staff in this respect. Information must be accurate, complete and timely.

Managers can take the active or passive view to information dissemination, the latter assuming that if people want to find out about something it is their responsibility. However, workers will seek information and feedback from numerous sources, including the formal organization, supervisors and co-workers in an attempt to reduce uncertainty and insecurity. In this environment rumour and hearsay flourish on the grapevine and can result in entrenched attitudes and a resistance to any kind of change (Hannon, 1982) but prompt, accurate and frank notification of developments can weaken the rumour mill, usually very active in a troubled organization

(Linquist, 1990). Providing information does much to avoid such rumours which are usually much worse that the reality anyway.

Another important point is that communication channels and systems must have the confidence of the staff. Despite efforts being made to pass information on through meetings, if the accuracy of the information is debatable, staff will be sceptical about whether they are being told the whole truth. Staff also resent being informed after the event:

> At the very last minute we find out, basically. We find out at the end when it's already been decided (library assistant, metropolitan borough).[3]

Although support staff often understand how much pressure senior management is under, they resent a lack of communication and, feeling left in the dark, can consider themselves victims of circumstance. When an organization is going through difficult times 'over-communicating' using multiple channels can help. Meetings should be reinforced by memos, bulletins, letters and e-mail if available. Reassurance and closer communications between management and support staff is imperative to gain a better understanding of what employees want and are concerned about, and can also reinforce 'esprit de corps'.

The aim should be to give library support staff a clear picture of how their authority and department is managed. Sudden changes of direction should not appear out of the blue. When the situation is changing rapidly, it is very difficult to keep staff up to date but providing regular information with opportunities for staff to contribute, or at least respond, to proposals will endow the communications network with greater credibility and encourage more confidence in management and its attempts to keep staff informed.

Consultation

As well as developing more effective ways of imparting downward communications, managers should also make an effort to establish systems which allow support staff to offer their opinions and which facilitate their input into the decision making process. Such systems can provide a basis for clarifying issues and can encourage support staff to feel that their managers are making more considered judgements as a result of information provided. Seeking employee input is more likely to elicit support for decisions as staff understand the rationale behind them.

An authoritarian climate in which managers make unilateral decisions and employees have no right of appeal is an important contributing factor to feelings of powerlessness and insecurity. Involving staff in the decision making process, however, can transform the management-worker relationship from a divisive contest over scarce resources to a joint effort to solve problems (Greenhalgh, 1984). Front-line support staff, being closest to the customer, are in a good position to suggest service improvements. Some of the most important insights into customer needs and service failing are to be found on the 'shop floor' (Line and Robertson, 1989) and this involvement can improve morale and develop self-confidence, self-esteem and new skills (Corrall, 1995). Just the fact that library assistants feel free to express opinions and know they will be considered can be motivation enough for many staff:

> I want my staff's opinion on everything. I find as a manager that all the staff here want to be involved in the progress and the success of the library, so I make an effort to involve them in almost every single aspect, right down to even budgeting. I say, 'It costs this much to run a library, we've got this much over, what do you reckon?' And I get a lot of feedback from them, they really enjoy it (librarian, London borough).[4]

Meetings in which everyone is encouraged to participate are an important way of gathering support staff opinions but informal methods can be just as important:

> Every time I walk through a room someone tells me something whether I want to hear it or not (librarian, county council).[5]

Even if there is no official forum in which assistants can air their views, a team structure can aid communications in this respect. In a close working team, assistants are encouraged to participate by chatting to their immediate supervisors and more senior managers. As the previous chapter discussed, the team system can often facilitate closer and more open relationships between the different grades of staff in which opinions can be expressed openly. Thus, restructuring can encourage a more relaxed atmosphere in which staff feel free to air their views on a daily basis, as part of the everyday running of their service points. A relaxed and receptive attitude to comments about the library, critical or otherwise, on the part of management is crucial to the success of such an open system.

An open-door policy is also important to encourage the views of those members of staff who do not like speaking out in front of others. Managers should emphasise to staff that, assuming they are available, support staff are welcome to approach them at any time to express their opinions or offer their suggestions. Time permitting, members of the library's management team can also go around to support staff individually from time to time, reinforcing the notion that there is always a senior member of staff available for them to see if they are unhappy about anything. More formal methods like employee suggestion schemes can also be useful ways of demonstrating that management values employees' suggestions and judgements.

Without official channels, the degree of consultation in libraries is very much dependent on the individual assistant's initiative, and on the personality and particular practices of individual line managers. Similarly, although meetings are a useful mechanism for discussion and dialogue in which support staff can air their views and any ideas they may have, their regularity and structure can vary considerably, reinforcing the suggestion that the management style of the individual in charge can be a crucially important factor in determining library assistants' working environment. As with information dissemination, although management intentions are often honourable as regards consulting staff, in practice the meetings system can fall down because of lack of time, pressure of work and the flexible working patterns of many library services.

Although there is no substitute for face-to-face communication and consultation, managers could consider other ways of gathering staff views. A questionnaire asking staff their opinions of the service and how they think it might be improved can be very effective, especially if anonymity is assured. Relatively simple acts like this can also generate large amounts of goodwill. Working parties, steering groups, consulting groups and workshops should all draw on all levels of staff, and can regularly change their membership so that everybody can have a chance to be involved. Although library assistants may initially feel intimidated and reluctant to speak up, assigning them at first to small group work and sub-groups can overcome their inhibitions.

Organizations can go to great lengths to involve their support staff, but it will have little effect if staff feel that, although their opinions are sought, their suggestions are rarely acted upon or their opinions taken into account:

> They do ask us [our opinion]. We have clerical staff meetings and they do ask us what we think. Whether they do anything about them is another thing (library assistants, county council).[6]

Staff can become frustrated if the consultative methods in place have little teeth and, again, resent being asked their opinion after decisions have been taken. The crucial factor in participation and consultation is how instrumental it is in achieving the employee's goals. When it results in major and direct changes then it can increase satisfaction with work. On the other hand, just providing a talking shop may have little positive effect on staff attitudes to their work, and can adversely affect them where the opportunities for consultation reveal limitations in influence (Greenhalgh, 1979). Thus, even when libraries do have formal ways of enabling library assistants' views to be heard, they do not always have the confidence of staff:

> It usually takes us all to make a big rumbling before anything's done. Sometimes you just feel worthless, I just don't feel that your views are counted or that you're ever consulted. I think there ought to be a lot more consultation because the library assistants really know about the library. We had one staff meeting which was supposed to be for the library assistants but they didn't really listen to what we thought. They really ought to listen more to the library assistants. We deal with the public, we deal with the system, we could give a lot of good input into how to work it but we're never asked (library assistant, county council).[7]

Negative attitudes like these can be minimised by ensuring that the decision making process is informed, fair and consultative. Management must be visible, honest and supportive during these difficult times. Informal consultation can establish confidence among staff and although management may not always feel employee input is strictly necessary, it is still beneficial to seek it as it encourages communications and will have a positive effect on staff/management relations.

Participation

It is to be hoped that restructuring has encouraged library managers to become more open, participative and consultative, giving staff the impression that they are now working in a far more relaxed environment. The team approach is increasingly becoming the norm and library managers frequently acknowledge that support staff from the backbone of library operations, and play a major role in the continuity and stability of library services with their intimate knowledge of their library, its stock and customers.

The broadening of the library assistant's role, responsibilities and skills has hopefully facilitated a change in management attitude towards this category of staff. As expectations of library assistants have risen, so managers should take the opportunity to take a serious look at the way support staff are expected to perform their jobs, what is now expected of them, the way those expectations are communicated and the way that they are recognised and rewarded. As library assistants take on more, and increasingly complex, tasks, it is likely that management will alter their views of support staff and their potential for involvement in the management of the service, their capacity for more skilled, demanding work and their entitlement to working conditions that satisfy their workplace and personal needs and ambitions. Libraries can no longer afford to distinguish between those who make decisions and those who implement them, and must find ways of effectively drawing ideas from the ranks to prevent the waste of intellectual capital.

Library assistants should be valued as part of the team with an important contribution to make to the service. A change of management style to one that is more prepared to talk to and consult staff has coincided with a new breed of assistant who wants to be involved more fully in the provision of the service. A readiness of managers to involve all levels of staff in team work is just one manifestation of this. Another is that managers are much friendlier, less aloof and more prepared to explain and discuss policies and issues. The role of the manager is moving much more towards that of facilitator, a team leader for the *full* team, not just professionals, who encourages ideas, contributions to debate and input into the decision making process from everybody

As the previous chapter noted, integration and discussion between the different categories of staff can take place on many levels, whether just in the day-to-day running of the service, in training sessions or in meetings. The restructuring of many library services, with paraprofessionals taking over the supervision of individual libraries, can promote a dialogue between support staff and their professionally qualified colleagues, making the latter much more willing to involve assistants in as many aspects of the running of the library as possible.

As managers become increasingly aware of the value of their support staff and the important role that they play, so this should lead to a change in the way work is organized with assistants becoming more fully integrated into the general management of the service. As staff without professional library qualifications take over the day-to-day running of the libraries, so there should be a greater willingness by management to recognise their skills and their value, and so they should be encouraged to take decisions about the service they provide the public.

Support staff often know how the organization can be improved, they have ideas about new services or about how an existing one could be improved, and can generally identify immediately why some intended change will not work. Yet often they take no action, do not offer their ideas and do not get involved. Managers who feel this is true of their support staff may try assessing their own, and their organization's, capacity for enquiry. It seems common sense to assume that those staff who perform a job are the most technically qualified to make decisions about it and how to improve it, and yet managers rarely tap that reservoir of experience and creative power.

Staff may feel that their questions will not be answered, and have little confidence that their new ideas will get fair consideration.

The move towards 'organic' management structures with flatter organizational hierarchies is gathering pace in library services, and has given individual service points in large systems considerable autonomy. Although this should result in enhanced user-oriented services, it is imperative that service priorities and long term strategic planning are safeguarded and this means that somebody has to have overall responsibility for managing the service. The process of gaining agreement for changes can be very cumbersome, however:

> I've moved to a new library. If I've got any ideas that I want put into practice I have to discuss it with the librarian. She discusses it with the community librarian who's her superior and the community librarian team leader discusses it with the group librarian. So there are quite a lot of decisions that I can't just make and put into practice, it all has to be agreed at different levels (paraprofessional, county council).[8]

Streamlining this process would do much to encourage support staff ideas who often feel frustrated that even minor decisions have to be referred upwards:

> Sometimes just little decisions where you think something might be improved, you think, 'Oh well, I'll just ask about this, if we can change it'. They say, 'Oh we'll have to discuss that at the area meeting' and you think, 'Well it's something that could be improved, I can't see why I can't just take it on myself to do' (library assistant, county council).[9]

Although larger decisions regarding individual library's operations should be discussed at a higher level, ensuring they comply with the service's overall objectives, there does seem to be a case for allowing assistants more freedom over their own working practices and procedures.

Library support staff often have knowledge, skill and expertise which is not used. They frequently feel over-worked, but at the same time they feel under-utilised. Staff often know how to improve what they do and may even, as managers of service points, have the freedom to do it. However, they may feel that they have never been given the go-ahead by management. A first step to encouraging support staff to become more involved in the management of the service is to ensure that people have the maximum control over their own jobs, as discussed in chapter 3. A second even simpler step is giving individuals the freedom to challenge the value, accuracy and usefulness of everything they do. This questioning can improve performance and management can guard against this process descending into biased nit-picking by insisting that staff have data to back up their opinions.

Staff should then be invited to suggest how they and their colleagues can best be organized to do their best work. Anyone doing a job for any length of time will find ways to improve it. Bottom-up participation must be stressed to re-energise people, to make them feel valued and to establish, or re-establish, trust. Although library managers generally recognise and value support staff for being at the sharp end of the service, and realise that they have to be supported if they are to work well, it seems that they often fail to communicate this to their staff. One way of expressing their appreciation is to give support staff more control over their work and more of a voice within the service.

However, the organization which is serious about introducing changes in participative practice and attitudes must invest heavily in training to facilitate the process. Increasing delegation and decentralisation must thus be accompanied by support and training to enable support staff to take on their new, more demanding roles.

Training and appraisal

As organizations undergo change and restructuring, individuals will almost certainly need new skills, but support staff training is one area where managers of libraries have not been creative. The restructuring of staff patterns has not been accompanied by a new imaginative stance on training policy. Training can alter staff attitudes towards innovation and change and can also be a valuable method of showing that the organization cares about its staff. Training and development activities can improve morale, help staff feel part of a team, and act as the 'glue' that keeps the organization together during major changes (Kiss, 1994).

Personnel development and training are potentially the most powerful tools for achieving organizational change. Training is concerned with learning the necessary practical skills to adjust to changing work patterns and requirements, and is also about altering people's attitudes so that they want to change and improve. Training can be thus either practical or attitudinal, i.e. training someone to do a job or task, or training someone to approach a situation in a positive way. Whatever the aim of training, however, it should be accompanied by a clear and acceptable appraisal system to identify developmental needs, and to communicate how well the individual is coping and performing in the new system.

The benefits that accrue to the organization with a well organized staff training and development programme have long been established. Not only do staff become more proficient, but staff morale and commitment are increased as the organization demonstrates that it is concerned about its staff and how they are developing. Employers have an obligation to provide opportunities for improvement, and staff development can make sure that staff are motivated, productive, and skilled in their jobs, and that they understand and can implement library purposes and policies (Conroy, 1978).

In a time of rapid change, the availability of high quality training and staff development for all staff becomes increasingly important (John Fielden Consultancy, 1993). A multitude of pressures, many of which were outlined in the introduction, is encouraging library employers to reassess their training provision. The introduction of quality initiatives and new technology have been particularly important factors in increasing the demand for training in libraries but, according to one survey (Personnel Management & Lloyds Masters Consulting, 1994), the greatest influence has been the drive to improve efficiency and performance in an ever more competitive and cost-conscious marketplace. In libraries this has led to major restructurings and changes in the way work is organized which in turn have required support staff to develop new skills to cope with new responsibilities.

Restructuring in libraries has led to fewer people doing more valuable work. The inevitable squeeze on support staff for increased productivity creates an obvious demand for skills development, and assistants are being forced to shoulder new responsibilities and acquire new skills to keep up with all the changes taking place in their organizations. Generally, these are 'home grown' people. Internal promotion of experienced employees is common, based on personal attributes, demonstrated ability and personality. It is important that training should support the development of this category of worker and their 'intermediate' skills. Their responsibilities in the areas of staff supervision, organization and co-ordination suggest that particular attention should be paid to these areas. It might be expected that training has become a priority in libraries, to prepare the more senior support staff for their new enlarged managerial responsibilities, and to give assistants in general the confidence to tackle their new duties with assurance.

Managers should be aware that assistants need more sophisticated skills and make efforts to provide their support staff with the training to ensure they are coping with the demands made upon them. However, managers often do not know what their assistants' training needs are and are unable to articulate them, which raises the important point of the extent to which the effectiveness and amount of training received by support staff is often reliant upon the motivation and commitment of the line manager.

Another important issue is whether the training and developmental activities available to support staff prepare them adequately for their jobs and give them the confidence to perform at their best. Money wasted on training is expensive and it is common for staff to be scheduled for training programmes that they did not select and in which they are not interested. Training needs should be established by extensive interaction with staff including individual and team analyses of what skills are needed now and will be needed in the future. A job/function task analysis will help ascertain the knowledge, skills and abilities required by support staff and, to ensure the relevance of training, staff could be asked to design their own training objectives, content and method of evaluation.

The training method must match the need. The 'sitting next to Nelly' approach to in-service training seems to be the method most often used, with support staff learning most of the skills and abilities needed in their posts solely on the job. Although the transfer of learning is maximised by this method, it can have drawbacks too. The training is often brief and unstructured; the trainer may find it a nuisance; and the trainee may be pressured to master the job too quickly. The new employee will also learn to do the job the way their supervisor does it which may not always be the most efficient. However, in-service training is critical to the development of quality public library services, and many of the skills needed by support staff can be better learnt through formal, properly structured in-service programmes rather than in the traditional classroom setting (Cevallos, and Kratz, 1990). Libraries should be encouraged to make extensive use of in-house experts and, to increase the reality of the situation, staff should preferably be trained as organizational units, i.e. with the people with whom they normally work and use their skills.

In-service training should be a constant strengthening process throughout the assistant's career (Larson, 1981). That training should be a continuous process, rather than a one-off exercise, is an important point, especially considering the rate of change in public library services, and the enlargement of many support staff roles and duties. Paraprofessionals appear to be on a constant learning experience as they adapt to the changing demands made on them and their libraries. This is not the same as continuous training, however. A comprehensive and properly structured in-service training programme would leave support staff better equipped to cope with the many changes their services are undergoing.

Specific skills training must be made available to support the changing activities of front line staff and NVQs could help as far as support staff are concerned. S/NVQs for the LIS sector were launched in 1995 and although it is too early to comment on their success or otherwise, in principle the Library Association welcomes their development which should provide a much needed structure for training and development for those without professional library qualifications (Dakers, 1995). These are competency-based qualifications which clarify the knowledge, skills and behaviours that make for the successful performance of the job. The qualification will be based on the identified competencies and skills needed to carry out specific jobs. Work-based assessment will be involved although knowledge-based learning will also have some part to play. By defining the job and individual tasks, with examples, support staff will be able to visualise what is expected of them to do a better job, to assess themselves against an ideal model and, with their supervisors, develop a plan of action that will help close the gap between current performance and ideal performance. NVQ may signal a change of attitude towards support staff training and may provide a more flexible answer to the problem of library assistants' qualifications.

S/NVQs thus offer the potential for a more highly organized, structured framework for support staff training especially for those who have been with their libraries for some years with little systematic developmental opportunities. However, the process of staff development should begin the day an individual accepts a position with the service. Few libraries, though, have 'orientation' or thorough induction programmes that ensure not only that employees are well versed in a particular task, but also have a sense of the institution as a whole. Such a programme can help the individual employee understand and 'internalise' the values of the service. Although these are clarified through the mission statement, training and induction will help transmit exactly what they mean to staff on a day-to-day basis. Induction training is thus not just about the nuts and bolts of the service, but should also transmit how different parts of the service operate and interact, helping the new employees understand their role and how it contributes to the overall aims of the organization.

Training should, thus, make an impact on the service, not just the individual. The aim is to make the organization more effective than it was before, and training should be a major part of how that is achieved. Training should enable support staff to keep their skills current and so contribute to the provision of a quality service. Continual attention to employee training at all levels make restructured services stronger and more able to cope with the demands made upon them.

The restructuring of staffing patterns and redefinition of roles within public library services give managers an ideal opportunity to reassess their training programmes and procedures. The relatively unorganized way in which the paraprofessional role developed gave management little time to formalise the different levels of work, or supervisory and managerial responsibilities into a sensible and coherent personnel structure, supported by a progressive programme of training and staff development which would give them the confidence to take on their expanded roles. It is now necessary to examine the organization as a whole. In general, coaching and training must be planned for and integrated into the total process of the management of change. Whole team training should also be considered, as an aid to service development and group cohesion.

Continuous planned training for all staff creates loyalty as well as ensuring that staff are prepared to meet the challenge of change. By emphasising training, the library stands a better chance of achieving its goals and although specific skills training is essential as roles, duties and ways of doing things change, training for change is also necessary to teach people to cope with the unexpected and new, and to encourage them to seize the opportunities the new climate can offer.

Training for change

Training for change concentrates on team work and team-building, stimulating genuine participation by staff in the processes of managing change and, in the process, increasing job satisfaction and productivity. Well-designed, but time-consuming and costly, training programmes can alter staff attitudes towards innovations. Most library managers seem to regard training merely as the transference of skills, to make assistants more competent and effective in their jobs. Although this is, of course, an important aspect of any training programme there are other benefits, and libraries that adopt S/NVQs must be careful not to neglect other forms of training.

Support staff often recognise and emphasise the importance of this side of training and appreciate that training activities are also a valuable way of showing the organization cares about its staff; that they can provide a boost to morale; and that they can help staff envisage themselves as part of a team:

> The thing with training courses is that I think sometimes people think the importance of them is in the actual training. The real importance of them is getting people together who rarely meet so they exchange ideas. And also people feel that somebody cares about them because they're training them and they're taking an actual interest in them (paraprofessional, metropolitan borough).[10]

Training and developmental activities can, thus, be stimulating and serve a greater purpose than merely the transference of skills or theories.

Training for change teaches staff to do things differently and think about the organization differently. Moving from traditional skills training to training for change requires different methods and a different use of training resources. Team-based training is all important with a focus on problem solving. The focus is on teams rather than upon the individual staff member as the object of training. Training for change involves giving staff the knowledge and skills to contribute fully to their work group and thus to the organization. It also equips individuals with the ability to respond and cope with the unexpected and new. Much of this learning can take place within daily work activities as long as all the members of the team are encouraged to contribute and play a full part in the provision of the service.

This type of training will partly focus on implementing new strategies that have already been decided upon, and partly on bringing fresh ideas and perspectives into the organization. Training and developmental strategies should be top priority for all library services who want to increase employee involvement and build strong teams in an attempt to enhance their reputation with the user. By focusing on employee development, the service can acquire competitive advantage by giving workers the skills which will be needed in the future.

It is important that any training offered or proposed has the support and interest of staff. Glogoff and Flynn (1990) recommend some sort of training needs assessment instrument, not only to assess staff strengths and deficiencies but also to ask staff to identify training techniques that had worked for them and those that had not. Inviting participation in formulating training plans in this way can help secure grass-roots support for any initiatives and can also be used to solicit the degree of interest for workshops on various topics. Appraisal schemes can also help identify training needs as well as open a dialogue with staff about their performances.

Appraisal and feedback

The importance of downward information dissemination was stressed above. A very important aspect of this is individual feedback from line manager to support staff member. Being appreciated by one's supervisor can make a significant contribution to employee contentment. When the supervisor demonstrates that s/he values and respects the individual staff member's opinion and takes an interest in his or her development and problems, then the employee feels s/he matters to the library. It is also impossible to perform adequately without regular feedback.

Feedback is seen as a necessary factor in work by those who emphasise the importance of higher order needs for self-esteem and self-actualisation (Ilgen et al, 1979). Appraisal procedures and feedback can also encourage a rapid flow of information throughout the system and establish confidence and credibility (Odini, 1990). Few library services have appraisal systems for their assistants, however. Although managers would like to see more formal appraisal systems being developed, the effort, time and training they involve means that their introduction has often been left on a back boiler. This can mean that the amount of feedback assistants receive is dependent, once again, on the personality, practices and individual policies of the line manager. In this situation, there is a danger that assistants never receive encouragement or performance feedback:

> The comments I've had twice are 'If you do something wrong, you'd know about it', which is a bit frustrating (paraprofessional, metropolitan borough).[11]

Managers should try to balance constructive criticism with praise and recognise employees' contribution to the organization (Jacobs, 1988). Staff appreciate a balance of praise and correction. They want to know if they are doing something wrong or if there is some way their performance can be improved but discipline, unmitigated by praise and regular positive feedback, can be disheartening and frustrating. Staff welcome any indication that they are performing their various tasks adequately. The lack of information about how an individual is progressing at work can be taken as a sign that supervisors take little notice of their support staff colleagues and are unconcerned about their work and their welfare. Assessment procedures imply a caring attitude and interest in what is being done and how. A lack of evaluation can be interpreted as indifference and disinterest in the growth of the individual staff member (Maehr, 1989).

Bywaters (1988) maintains that after reorganization a performance appraisal system should be implemented in which each employee is clear about how they are doing in their restructured jobs, how they might improve, what is expected of them and what they can expect in return. Feedback may be especially important for paraprofessionals in the wake of restructuring, many having taken on a considerable increase in responsibility. For an initial period they may need an increased amount of feedback and reassurance that they are performing competently in their new enlarged posts.

In these circumstances, positive feedback is particularly important to reassure staff. Staff will appreciate being told in concrete and specific terms that they are doing a good job and performing their work competently. Feedback should concentrate on telling individuals how fully their performance is meeting expectations and what impact their behaviour and performance is having on the service. Informal feedback can be given in many situations and at any time, and although this informal, spontaneous feedback can be a huge morale booster, ideally feedback should be structured because there is a danger that without a formal system, good intentions fall by the wayside. Feedback should be concrete and specific, focusing on information that can be understood and acted upon. It should also be limited to a certain number of topics to avoid information overload and subsequent inaction. Finally, feedback should be timely and given at the appropriate time and place.

In libraries, feedback is most likely to be immediate, informal and specific. This is all very well when supervisors work alongside their assistants. However, increasingly support staff, notably paraprofessionals, are being left in sole charge of service points. These staff often feel that most of the time they are virtually working independently. Performance feedback and praise in these circumstances can be lacking. Although these staff have superiors that they have to answer to, their contact with them is such that regular feedback is rare.

A more standard approach to feedback would improve communications in library services. Although an appraisal system would have to be promoted positively and sensitively so that staff would not regard it as 'the annual telling off', assistants should welcome the chance to open a regular, systematic dialogue about their performance with their supervisors. The establishment of more formal channels for feedback would also help remedy the rather patchy picture that currently exists. The introduction of regular, official appraisal systems would ensure that supervisors who rarely give feedback are made aware of its importance and would be compelled to think about recognising their staff's contribution. It would also help identify any training needs as well as being an important indication of how much management values its staff and cares about their development. Milestones, rating systems, peer reviews and self-assessment are all useful ways of evaluating staff performance. Whatever the system used, it has to have the acceptance of the staff.

Appraisals are often considered intricate, time-consuming, harrowing and sometimes traumatic experiences by both supervisors and the supervised. However, appraisals should hold no surprises for the individual being assessed and there are various methods that can be used to ensure appraisals are viewed with less trepidation. Firstly, the purpose of the appraisal should be clear and acceptable to all. Ideally, performance review and developmental plans for the individual should be dealt with separately but pressure of time means that they are usually handled together. Self-assessment is a useful way of encouraging staff to look at their own performance and start a dialogue about their achievements. Staff should also be encouraged to identify where they need improvement and even suggest action they might take to remedy any deficiencies. In this way appraisal becomes much less of a one-sided affair controlled by management. Staff can identify the type of feedback they need and find most useful; how it should be given; and when. The process should be mutually agreed between supervisor and support staff member including what should be covered, and the sequence of issues. Goal setting, too, should be a joint effort. Finally, the appraisal process itself should be appraised by staff to determine if, and how, the process can be improved.

The idea that staff can challenge library systems and accepted ways of doing things can be as much of a shock for them as their supervisors, but it is essential that they are given a voice. Whether they take advantage of it or not depends on how well management handles the quite considerable cultural change restructuring entails.

Organizational culture

Organizational culture is an important indicator of success. Acceptance or otherwise of the culture can determine staff satisfaction and productivity and also the public's impression of the library. Organizational culture must be nurtured carefully and continually. However, the entire culture of the service sector is changing dramatically and if not handled sensitively the changes can lead to poor staff morale and a decline in productivity. It is essential that managers develop and articulate exactly what the library is trying to do and how staff contribute to organizational objectives. The aim should be to harness support staff acceptance and even enthusiasm for the changes taking place. Luckily for the management of library and information services, their assistants have shown themselves to be amenable to change in both organizational structure and culture.

Support staff have reacted with remarkable equanimity to the changing library service environment. In the wake of restructuring, for example, they frequently perceive a chance to improve their positions and their jobs, and take on board the considerable changes this entails for the content and responsibility of their work with little fuss. Management must find a way of taking advantage of their acceptance of change, by ensuring that support staff can clearly identify the advantages for themselves or the service which will result.

A major issue in the management of public library services in the late 1980s and early 1990s was the introduction of increasing fines and charges for services. This subject will be used as a case study to illustrate how, with management support, library support staff can change their views and reconcile themselves to even accepting an erosion of a concept at the heart of the public service ethos and culture.

It is apparent from the discussion in previous chapters that support staff enter public library work because they have a sense of public duty and are committed to the underlying mission and ethos of the service. However, as well as pressure to keep down costs, the last sixteen years have also seen the encouragement of the public sector to raise money. For some staff members these issues may be a matter of conscience. Many have a deep faith in an institution which exists to serve the needs of the whole community and endeavours to make information freely accessible to all. Some feel there has been an alarming tendency to dismiss these principles as unrealistic in the present climate and oppose charging and income generation believing they limit access and availability (e.g.Usherwood, 1989; King, 1989). Others do not consider libraries an appropriate area for the exercise of financial market signals (Line and Scott, 1989).

It has been argued that an increasing emphasis on money and fund-raising may decrease job satisfaction for some staff and cause role conflict (Nauratil, 1989) and stress (Lambert, 1985). Fees and charges can also strain staff/user relationships or at least change their nature as money is now passed over the counter. There is a danger that the income gained will not offset the effects of this change in the character of the service and the loss of public support for libraries that fees and increased charges will prompt (Govan, 1988).

However, the data gathered for the study on which this book is based suggest that those initially wary of charging have been won over. Many in the public library service have modified or compromised their free service philosophy to adopt one of cost recovery which they feel can help foster the development of a more active role and attitude. Staff feel that in an era of decline a judicious use of fees is appropriate and take the view that, in the practical world, principle must frequently be tempered by expediency where a library is faced with the simple choice of either charging for special services or not offering them at all. As table 5.1, shows the majority of respondents in the study reported here agreed to some extent that charges benefit the library, the greatest support for the statement being in the ranks of library assistants. Staff feel that charging for services offers a little bit more financial security in an environment where demands for cost effectiveness and efficiency are increasing. Charges can diversify a library's sources of income and make them less dependent on institutional funding. Charges are viewed as a necessity to keep services running, people in jobs and books on shelves.

Table 5.1
Responses to statement, 'Charges benefit the library'

	paraprofessionals	library assistants
strongly agree	5%	0%
agree	67%	78%
neither agree nor disagree	19%	7%
disagree	10%	15%
strongly disagree	0%	0%

Fees and income generation schemes are occasionally viewed as more bother than they are worth, but there is an acceptance that, increasingly, this is the direction in which the public library service is moving:

> Well, it's just the way of the world now. I don't see why we should be any different so long as it's not charging people coming in the doors or particularly high charges for reservations, but for specialist services people very often say, 'Is there a charge for that?' and we say no. So I don't see why not, as long as it's not exorbitant. It is the way of things now (paraprofessional, metropolitan borough).[12]

However, although agreeing in principle with the idea of charging, support staff feel that only certain services should be charged for. Charging for audio-visual services, reservations and company information for businesses is quite acceptable and it is generally felt that if these services can be run to make a bit of profit that can be ploughed back into the stock fund then all well and good. Support staff feel that income generation makes it easier to pay the bills and that their futures become more secure because of the additional income. Services can be expanded, maintained or even initiated.

The accuracy of these claims are debatable and it could be argued that libraries are exchanging one kind of dependency for another by abandoning their position of being reliant on public funding for dependence on external funds. As library services earn more, so the council may feel justified in reducing their contribution and so libraries may be caught in a vicious circle where they have to find increasingly large amounts from external sources. Moreover, the revenue raised often goes into the authority's Treasury coffers rather than back into a library fund. There is also the danger that libraries will be tempted to take the small step from selling library service to those who can afford them or who are prepared to pay for them, to actually seeking out paying customers and this will not benefit the vast majority of users because it will divert funds and staff away from other core services and could result in an imbalance where library resources are unfairly distributed to attract and service paying customers. The amount of money involved in setting up and running income generating services is another factor sometimes not taken into account.

However, this is not the place to rehearse these arguments. The important point is that support staff believe that charging, fines and income generation benefit the library by supplementing library budgets. There is a feeling that without the money from income generation activities, other services would suffer and that as long as public libraries provide the basic library service free, then that is acceptable. Support staff often protest that they would hate to see fees for the borrowing of books or the provision of information to the public indicating that there are deep philosophical objections to the idea of abandoning the free public library service and a belief that every avenue should be tried before that. However, it is often argued that to maintain a free core library service, 'extra' services have to be charged for:

> You can't be expected to have all the extra services without having to pay for them because they do cost money and if you want to keep the basic library service free for everyone then extra things, that not everybody would want, just perhaps a few would want, then they should perhaps pay for them (library assistant, county council).[13]

The general feeling among public library support staff is thus that some services should be provided according to the users' willingness to pay while maintaining a basic level of service for those unwilling or unable to pay. Flynn (1990) refers to this as the 'residualisation' of public services whereby those who are relatively well off and are able and willing to pay obtain a higher level of service while 'the rest' have to put up with,

> ...reduced funds, tight budgets and a minimalist attitude to service provision and investment (Flynn, 1990, p. 174).

This change in culture has met little active resistance among support staff, most accepting the modern 'mixed economy' operating in their public library services. Although in the 1980's the largest and most influential force in the Library Campaign was support staff, protesting against cuts and closures, few in this group are now concerned with protesting against cuts and fees for services but rather with making the current system with its mixture of free and fee more effective and socially acceptable. In the terms of Kurt Lewin's 'Force Field Theory', the situation was 'unfrozen' in the late 1980's when the government green paper on public library finance (Financing Our Public Library Service, 1988) was published and regarded as a major turning point for public libraries. At that time fears for the future of the free public library service were voiced from all quarters of the library community. Objections were raised, questions were asked and defences marshalled. However, the situation appears to have now 're-frozen' with increasing charges, fines and new charged-for services accepted by most of those who have to actually administer them: the support staff.

It would have been thought that there were considerable 'restraining forces' which would have encouraged support staff to take a dim view of this huge change to the public library culture. Apart from the points against it raised above, charges are a potential barrier to use of a library's service at whatever level they are set and will always give certain individuals pause for thought as to whether they are going to make use of a service or not. Charges can deter people from using a service and cause considerable resentment:

> I think people are very unwilling to actually pay for their service. If it's free that's fine and they'll use it but I think if you start charging a lot for the services we offer or for our time in looking for things I think people will stop using the library as much. I think you have to put it down to a public service (library assistant, county council).[14]

Increased charges and fines can also make work generally more difficult for the staff who have to collect them. Newly imposed or a raised level of charge can cause counter disputes and it is the staff at service point level who take the flak. Each new charged-for service means more work for assistants as well. There is also the view that having goods for sale does not do the image of the library any good, 'cheapening' it and causing stress and friction across the circulation desk.

The challenge for management in these circumstances is to present a positive image of charges for services and income generation. The 'driving forces', i.e. the benefits of these activities, have to be clearly spelled out if support staff are going to engage in them willingly and wholeheartedly. Staff may be unhappy with a commercial approach and the issue needs to be handled with care.

The main strategy adopted is to show support staff how their particular libraries can benefit, and support staff do appear to have taken this message to heart, believing that without fund raising activities the service would not be able to afford to buy or replenish stock, and that anything that generates income for this purpose is beneficial for the library and for the public who are thus given a better service. It is argued that it is quite legitimate to capitalise upon the willingness of certain sections of the library-using public to pay for improved or 'extra' services. The money gained through such enterprises is seen as supporting the library's other functions, or as a means to continue developing to attract even more readers.

Income generating services can also be used to encourage non-users into the library, and can improve the image of the library presented to the public:

> I think we've probably got more readers in to look at the videos and from there to look at the books, so I think it's actually increased our readership (library assistant, London borough).[15]

In other cases, the 'driving force' or rationale behind management's promotion of income generation has a *negative* aspect; i.e. if the library service does not raise more of its income from external sources service points will close and jobs will be lost. In these circumstances, although initially income generation was welcomed as a way of providing additional resources for libraries, it has now become an essential part of the budget. The emphasis has changed. Whereas previously income generation was promoted because of the extras it could provide, it is now endorsed because the service could probably not survive without it. The message that managers increasingly seem to be sending out to their staff is that the more income libraries can generate, the more it helps the budget overall, and the fewer jobs or services will be lost. Hardly a positive message but one that strikes a chord with many of their support staff:

> We feel in this economic climate it keeps us all employed (paraprofessional, London borough).[16]

Thus, management can present a change, which theoretically questions some of the fundamental principles of the public library service, in a positive light and although this is a dramatic example of how a change to organizational culture can be effected through careful re-positioning and reinforcement of a message, smaller, less significant changes can also be handled in this way. Support staff generally seem amenable to change. For them, issues are decided on their merits with little room for ideology. They are in favour of what works best in any given situation, and combine a concern with effectiveness and efficiency with a desire for a responsive and

117

sensitive service. With careful management, change can be harnessed as opportunity and the threat of change can be converted into productive and profitable actions.

Conclusions

Previous chapters have outlined the exciting possibilities that change and restructuring hold for support staff and the library services that employ them. However, there are many challenges that management must face. One of these is a change of attitude to recognise the abundance of talent in the ranks of which they can take advantage. Changes in organizational design can encourage better communications and decision making at all levels. This must be backed up by a supportive organizational culture which encourages staff to question procedures and policies, while reinforcing the key values of the service. Management needs to develop and articulate exactly what the service is trying to accomplish.

Library managers should be ready to listen to and involve their support staff. The onus is very much on management to acknowledge the value of their support staff and provide training and development for them. Education and training can help the individual understand how their individual work relates to the overall goals of the service. A quality service depends on the commitment of every individual in the workforce and this in turn is dependent upon the development of a properly resourced and planned training programme which is implemented in line with, and evaluated against, organizational goals. This necessitates the formulation of job appraisal schemes and skills audits, comprehensive induction arrangements, and the training of line managers in human resource development functions.

Change is an unsettling process. It can undermine self-confidence and erode the quality of working life. Change, therefore, requires face-to-face management of the highest order and managers should ensure that they are giving and receiving feedback, and entering into open discussion with their staff. Constant reinforcement of the message that management appreciates and values the work of staff in these circumstances is essential.

However, while uncertainty continues to be the order of the day managers will be tempted to react negatively, focusing primarily on the short term. In these circumstances management must take care that reorganization and change does not undercut long term employee training needs. Despite the need for better training programmes to create more skilled workers, libraries are, in fact, often cutting back on staff and relying more on part-time and temporary workers who receive little or no formal training. These changes in employment patterns, to be discussed in the next chapter, could negatively impact upon the long term quality of the library workforce.

Notes

1. Goulding, A. (1993), *Managing Public Library Support Staff in Times of Change,* p. 436
2. Ibid, p. 438
3. Ibid, p. 441
4. Ibid, p. 447
5. Ibid, p. 447
6. Ibid, p. 454
7. Ibid, p. 456
8. Ibid, p. 414
9. Ibid, p. 415
10. Ibid, p. 509
11. Ibid, p. 426
12. Ibid, p. 339
13. Ibid, p. 353
14. Ibid, p. 342
15. Ibid, p. 356
16. Ibid, p. 379

6 Workforce planning and equal opportunities

Library managers today do not have the luxury of working in a stable, predictable environment as economic, political and social changes impact on their organizations, demanding a positive response. After restructuring, managers need to review the mixture of skills and experience in their libraries to create a degree of stability and ensure achievement of organizational goals. Workforce planning is the procedure of matching staffing resources to service needs. A reassessment of the priority of services provided might also be necessary which will again affect the kinds of skills needed in the organization as staff are shifted from low priority to high priority areas. In response to external and internal change, library organizations have been reducing expenses, reorganizing operations and cutting the workforce. Having reached 'core' staffing levels, one method of continuing to increase efficiency and productivity is to turn to flexible working patterns. The increasing use of flexible workers has important implications for conditions of work and equality of opportunity in the workplace.

This chapter outlines the implications of restructuring and change for library employers' workforce strategies, in particular the effects on:

- workforce planning;
- libraries' use of flexible work patterns;
- equal opportunities for women support staff.

Workforce planning

Workforce planning involves various tasks and techniques which are meant to ensure that the right type of staff are in the right jobs at the right time (Zeffrane and Mayo, 1994). Current levels of staff and skills have to be analysed to assess if they match the needs of the service and the needs of the user, now and in the future. Workforce planning is a system of monitoring and managing the flow of staff in, through and out of the organization to ensure that it is continuing to provide an effective service through the recruitment and retention of staff with the necessary skills mix to achieve service objectives. Workforce planning is thus concerned with meeting the necessary changes in the volume, flow and skills profile of the staff of the organization.

Change and restructuring result in enormous changes to the make-up of the workforce and the relationships between different sections of the organization. The restructuring of library workforces in the face of economic and political change has resulted in streamlining, elimination and reshuffling of staff, in the belief that these strategies will help reduce costs and create a more flexible service. However, they have also often resulted in 'restructuring disfunctions' (Zeffrane and Mayo, 1994). These could include a rise in conflict between different departments or sections in a library as certain units seem to get a larger share of resources (staff and materials) than others:

> The branch libraries get very, very angry because nobody seems to care about us. We are of little significance. The only people that really matter are Central, so there's a great deal of resentment about that (paraprofessional, metropolitan borough).[1]

The dismantling of both formal and informal networks that help organizations run smoothly might also cause long term problems including serious declines in service quality if management does not make the effort to analyse the work activities and skills of the staff who are due to be reorganized, leading to missed opportunities and unhappy users. Unplanned workforce restructuring can give rise to reduced co-ordination and co-operation between sections, and bring development to a halt. Thus, the effectiveness of the service can be easily eroded by short-sighted retrenchment techniques (Levine, 1984). Broad scale, unplanned and unco-ordinated restructuring can weaken staff capacity and effectiveness.

The emergence of the paraprofessional could be said to be a direct result of libraries' workforce planning strategies which have often resulted in adjustments to the ratio of professional to support staff. Library services have generally opted for a small core of highly experienced, highly flexible staff who need minimal supervision, supported by a larger pool of less highly trained staff who can be hired at less cost. However, care needs to be taken in assessing the impact on the service of trade-offs between professional and support staff reductions as they may have long term implications for the capacity of the organization to deliver its services.

Organizational and environmental changes affect the organization's personnel plan and organizations facing change need a supportive workforce plan. Restructuring in library services has often meant staffing cuts but major reductions in the workforce can put the organization at risk as it has to fulfil its obligations with a smaller and probably weaker workforce. Organizing a smaller staffing establishment to ensure that the library is meeting its service objectives is complex. The challenge is to reshape the organization to ensure that staffing resources are concentrated on the most necessary parts of the service and perhaps contracting the number of staff on those operations considered to be less important to the service's overall mission. The key is ensuring that the right mix of skilled and motivated workers are in the right places at the right time.

Chapter 4 outlined how staffing cutbacks have increased the work for many on the front-line of library services. Where and how cuts are made can make all the difference to the effectiveness of services. Staff in large, busy libraries often feel under considerable pressure and contrast their high-stress working environment with other units in the organization where life seems a lot slower. The former feel they are never able to get on top of the work. A change in demands for certain types of service may also mean that some sections become busier than others:

> I think since we've had the AV collection in the libraries there's been a lot more pressure at the counter and no extra staff (library assistant, metropolitan borough).[2]

In libraries there are obvious fluctuations in job load: sometimes an assistant is busy, other times s/he has little to do. Managers must try to forecast the demand for each service and thus each type of employee and identify which can be shifted from low-demand to high-demand assignments. This involves gathering supply and demand data and comparing them to develop a workforce plan which assesses current and future staffing needs, and takes action to meet those needs. Systematic planning can help managers decide which jobs are vital to the library service and which types of jobs could be eliminated.

Management must be sure to keep staff informed at all times about the workforce planning process. A review of positions and jobs within the organization might provoke fears related to job security but a clear explanation from management can do much to allay fears. By ensuring the process is open and consultative, at least staff can be sure that the review is not being undertaken in an perfunctory manner within a managerial vacuum.

The aim should be to identify trends and changes that will affect the service and calculate their implications for staffing needs. Decisions need to be taken on how to fill critical positions in the organization, whether to acquire new staff or train and develop existing employees. Time should be spent filling these positions with the right people, who might very well already be within the organization. However, although it is vital that library services anticipate their staffing resources in terms of size and composition, formal strategic workforce planning can be neglected because of other demands on management's time:

> ...very often, in making their plans for the future, organizations don't give enough thought to the preparation and development of their people ... Those who lead organizations are used to setting objectives. They are used to thinking ahead. But how many plans include people, other than the staffing required at a managerial level? (quoted in: John Fielden Consultancy, 1993).

Organizations thus need to plan for the people who will put their strategic plans into effect. However, very often a long term staffing strategy is neglected in times of change as pressures and crises encourage managers to focus on short term exigencies. Recruitment freezes and voluntary redundancy programmes have frequently been the methods that library organizations have used to reorganize their staffing structures. They may now be paying the price as services and long term planning suffer because of the lack of strategic focus and the lack of experienced managers and employees. This can be exacerbated by the increasing use of flexible workers.

In an attempt to achieve flexibility, there is a danger that library services are travelling too far down the part-time and temporary staffing road:

> You have an awful lot of people who are working part-time because it's very convenient and it's close to home in convenient hours. We can be so flexible, we can just about suit anybody's strange family commitments, or whatever. But the bottom line on that is that you're creating a difficult line through the organization. People who find it convenient to work in one library, even if you've got a better graded post elsewhere, are not likely to strive for it. You can build in a complacency and a lack of flexibility. If you're looking for the next manager and you're pulling from a low hours, I-don't-want-move workforce, then it's quite difficult (senior manager, county council).[3]

Thus, some library services might be storing up trouble for themselves in their eagerness to recruit flexible staff for economy and flexibility reasons, especially at a time when the trend is for support staff to take over many of the administrative and managerial tasks and responsibilities once undertaken by professionally qualified librarians. Without a pool of committed, highly trained, ambitious assistants to draw upon, many library organizations may find themselves severely bereft of supervisory talent. However, there is no reason why support staff in less than full-time posts should not advance into supervisory positions. It is the responsibility of the management of library services to ensure that all staff have the necessary training, development and support that will equip them for higher level posts. If managers take the attitude that flexible workers cannot work in supervisory positions, the workers themselves are likely to be of the same opinion and the organization is in danger of wasting a huge pool of talent and experience. Imagination and commitment is needed to manage the flexible workforce sensitively and to ensure that it is used to best effect for the good of the library and its users.

Flexibility

All organizations need to match their staffing needs with labour supply. In library services that supply seems to be increasingly found in the pool of flexible workers. A recent major survey of flexible working patterns in libraries highlights the importance of part-time, temporary and casual workers, with managers often describing them as "vital" to their organization's ability to operate (Goulding and Kerslake, 1995). The survey also found that flexible working schedules were particularly prevalent among support staff.

Flexible workers may be defined as workers who engage in any of the following:

> ...non-permanent work, work without employee status and work
> with short or irregular hours (Huws et al, 1989, p. 20).

They may also be workers whose place of work is variable. Staff who work on permanent part-time, temporary part-time, job-share, homeworking, temporary full-time, term-time and annualised working hours' contracts make up the bulk of the flexible workforce in library services.

The last 20 years have witnessed a huge expansion in the use of flexible workers in all employment sectors, but particularly in the service sector. Within this expansion of the flexible workforce, the rapidly increasing numbers of part-time workers have been significant (Naylor, 1994). Information services have been no exception to this general trend. In libraries, where flexible workers have long been a substantial part of the workforce, the previous decade has seen their ever increasing deployment by managers.

The increase in flexible working patterns has particular significance for library and information services for a number of reasons.The demand for flexible forms of employment is highest among women, therefore the issues are particularly important for organizations where women form a significant proportion of the workforce, like libraries. Moreover, Fields and Thakur (1991) suggest that some types of work may be better suited to part-time employment than others, and library work is arguably one of these. There is considerable scope for part-time work in libraries. The variable working hours and work loads of library services make part-time work very attractive from the employer's viewpoint.

Increasing demand for information services has been accompanied by recession, spending restrictions and recruitment difficulties in some regions. Demographic changes have altered the make up of the labour force, with a vast increase in the numbers of married women once again participating (Beechey and Perkins, 1989) accounting for a large increase in job-share posts. Thus, in response to changes over the last decade, libraries, like other employment sectors, have increasingly adopted flexible working patterns in an attempt to retain control over their staffing establishments.

Flexible working schedules have always enabled library and information organizations to manage daily and weekly peaks and troughs in demand for services, but now they also allow managers to cope with budgetary uncertainty and impending change, such as local government reorganization. Flexibility today plays a dual role in library and information services enabling managers to cover evening opening hours, for example, and, more bleakly, to cope with zero jobs growth policies. Information services should therefore be aware of the dangers of choosing the "low road" to flexibility via short term cost cutting measures, rather than investing in the "high road" with its associated investment and long term perspective (Harrison, 1993).

Thus, two discrete forces appear to be behind these innovations in workforce strategies. External economic circumstances mean that part-time and temporary contracts are very attractive to hard-pressed library managers trying to trim their wages budgets. An internal pressure of staff demand is also encouraging more libraries to adopt flexible working patterns. However, it has been argued that if the 1970's were characterised by a growth in *employees'* working time flexibility, the 1980's and 1990's have witnessed the emphasis shifting to *employers'* desire to secure greater temporal flexibility (Blyton, 1994) as the introduction of new technology and the subsequent changes in work organization, combined with the need to cut labour costs, put a premium on securing maximum value from the labour force.

Management-led initiatives to introduce flexible working patterns have established alternatives to full-time employment as an important facet of library managers' labour use strategies. Managers have worked with flexible working patterns to prove that they can be a dynamic force in taking a fresh look at workforce planning policies and practices, while also tackling old problems for staff struggling to reconcile their domestic and work roles.

The evidence suggests that the flexible library workforce is primarily employer-led and exists for the convenience of the organization. In the survey of flexible working patterns mentioned above, respondents were asked their reasons for employing flexible workers. The given choices were:

- staff retention;
- ability to manage workloads;
- to meet staff demand;
- unavailability of staff;
- to reduce staffing costs;
- to increase productivity;
- to ensure weekend cover;
- the post did not require a full-time worker;
- to reduce absenteeism;
- to reduce staff turnover; and,
- to increase the range of skills among staff.

The most common responses were to manage variable workloads; to ensure cover for weekend opening hours; and to retain valued staff. However, the balance between employer-led grounds for using flexible workers in library and information services and employee-led grounds is in a state of flux dependent on both the demographic and economic climate (Wallis, 1990; Auckland, 1990; Morris, 1990).

Financial uncertainty, for example, has a major impact on libraries' labour use strategies. Because of budgetary constraints, managers are increasingly reluctant to make permanent agreements with new staff. Increasingly, therefore, libraries are turning to temporary and casual staff. The potentially exploitative nature of these types of contract should be borne in mind, however. Casual workers in libraries are rarely guaranteed the number of hours they work in any week or month, and therefore the amount of pay they earn is uncertain. They also do not receive holiday or sickness pay. The increasing use of casual workers appears to support the argument put forward by Huws et al (1989) that the term "casualisation" should be used instead of "flexibilisation" in labour market terminology. Library Managers also use temporary staff to enhance numerical staff flexibility, that is to cope with variable, but perhaps short-lived, needs for changing numbers of staff.

This might include covering for staff on training courses, for staff off sick, or for staff on secondment.

Libraries thus employ flexible workers for a vast range of reasons. Generally flexible working patterns are considered beneficial as they provide the organization with increased flexibility in staffing patterns and offer many, especially married women, the opportunity to take on a job while still fulfilling other obligations or pursuing other interests. It should be remembered, though, that while the individual and social benefits gained from the availability of flexible working schedules are often enumerated by managers, most of these positions are created by library managers in response to a squeeze on funding and technological change which make operating efficiency and cost reduction essential.

While some flexible workers enjoy their fairest terms and conditions ever as a result of legislation in February 1995, managerial sympathies with some working patterns appear to be wearing thin, although managers often report being satisfied with the way permanent and temporary part-time workers and job-sharers work in their organizations. However, the logistical and operational problems associated with managing flexible workers are making some managers think twice about the value of a flexible workforce.

Managers might regard the logistics of co-ordinating work and meetings for flexible workers as aggravating. Obviously by using flexible workers instead of full-time staff, the number of individuals in the organization can double, meaning there are a lot of bodies to look after. As well as the increased administration workload, the organization also increases its training needs. The cost of the training, together with the practicalities of finding suitable times, or methods of paying people for training in time outside their normal working hours, can be problematic.

Communication is a commonly cited problem associated with managing flexible workers and insofar as it relates to staff meetings this is also linked to issues around co-ordination. The difficulties of incomplete communication, where a worker has not attended a meeting and is given a memorandum instead is another problem which will not only leave flexible workers feeling they have missed out, but might also have implications for the effectiveness of the service. Large numbers of flexible staff can also make it difficult for managers to offer an appropriate amount of management time for communicating with individuals. Organizational failure to manage flexible workers sensitively will have a serious impact on the motivation and productivity of the workers involved.

Faced with these difficulties, managers might be less sympathetic to flexible workers who have elected their working pattern (such as job-sharers), than those who have responded to an employer-led initiative (such as advertising for temporary staff). As job-sharing is such an important way for women, and in particular women with dependent children, to maintain (if not advance) their status in the labour market when they have caring responsibilities, a negative reception of this form of working is extremely worrying, and discriminatory.

The decision to implement flexible working patterns should only be the start of an organization's consideration of the matter, and the consequent implications should be addressed, rather than left for the individual worker and line manager to resolve as best they can. In order to gain a fuller understanding of flexible working patterns, managers must separate the logistical issues associated with these workers, such as communication and co-ordination, from strategic staff management issues.

Flexible workers are caught in a contradiction created by employers. Employers make use of flexible working patterns to achieve organizational strategic and operational aims, such as reducing labour costs, increasing productivity and staffing opening hours, as noted above. At this point, blatantly or more subtly, however, employers and managers contradict themselves. Once flexible workers are in post, *employee-led* reasons for not working full-time (i.e., to accommodate caring responsibilities, to allow time for study and so on) are attributed to them by managers. For example, managers might maintain that the use of job-share workers is "for their convenience, not ours".

This conflation of employer-led and employee-led reasons for flexible working is damaging to flexible workers. It maintains, legitimises and attempts to excuse the lower status, remuneration, training and promotion opportunities accorded to flexible workers, while still allowing managers to achieve organizational aims and enabling them to promote their organization as 'family friendly' and progressive. The existence of flexible workers indicates that there could be more to life than an eight-hour working day. However, this reference to the world beyond work is perceived as a lack of commitment to the company, as though the employee is not responsible enough to pursue company objectives. The yardstick against which flexible workers are being measured in this instance is full-time workers and flexible workers are often considered by managers to be sadly lacking.

Although managers believe that the use of flexible library staff promotes flexibility in the workplace, as noted above there is, nevertheless, anxiety over the future recruitment of assistants capable of being promoted to paraprofessional, supervisory posts. There is often a firmly held belief that managerial posts cannot be less than full-time. Part-timers in jobs where there are also full-time workers, are not considered as eligible for promotion. The exercise of authority is usually assumed to require full-time involvement with the job for reasons of continuity. However, it has been suggested that, in fact, the notion of *permanency* is crucial and that part-time permanent

128

employment could open up the possibility of career oriented part-time library support staff and the expansion of part-time opportunities in more skilled positions (Vincent, 1978).

Managers need to develop an understanding of flexible workers' demands and requirements. There is evidence that flexible workers have different reasons for working from their full-time colleagues, and presumably value different things in the workplace, as there is:

> ...some indication that the part-time worker is a different type of person from the full-time worker (Hall and Gordon, 1973, p. 47).

Different, however, should not mean, as it so often seems to, worse. Flexible workers can be a valuable asset to an organization, bringing new opportunities. To achieve this, organizations and managers need to manage them sensitively, appropriately and fairly, paying due regard to both the spirit and the letter of equal opportunities policies and laws. Thus, flexible working patterns offer opportunity but also they require careful planning if both employer and employee are to profit. The benefits of flexible working must be balanced against the new responses and skills demanded of managers. Having taken the plunge and decided to create such posts, managers must now take up the challenge they have set themselves.

Equal opportunities

Flexibility and equal opportunities

The overwhelming majority of flexible support staff workers in the library and information sector are women, thus issues relating to gender and equal opportunities are impossible to ignore. What happens if women, after a period of flexible work, later want to return to full-time working? Are there any penalties in taking the flexible option, perhaps in missed training or promotion opportunities, or decreased pension or welfare rights? Inevitably, one of the main and immediate consequences of flexible working, as opposed to full-time permanent working, is that it is a more poorly remunerated and often, although not always, a less secure form of employment. Combined, these issues could contribute to a perpetuation of women's economic dependence on men (Walby, 1990).

Employers may overtly or silently presume that because most library assistants are women, they are working only to bring a second wage into the family home and that the option of flexible working hours and part-time employment makes up for the low wages and lack of career structure.

Because of this, there is considerable ambivalence about the issue of part-time work. Although it could be argued that flexible working patterns that encourage women back to work are a 'good thing', unfortunately, flexible working schedules continue to be regarded as women's preserve reinforcing the traditional female/male stereotypical roles and division in the workplace. The eighth British Social Attitudes survey (Jowell et al, 1991) suggests that part-time work is often taken up from necessity rather than choice and that it often means downward mobility as the best jobs are mostly full-time. Thus, part-time work is probably a significant factor in the vertical occupational segregation of women.

Another potential difficulty that managers have to overcome is how to ensure that their flexible workers have access to appropriate training and developmental opportunities. The logistics of training provision can mean that flexible workers are excluded because training schedules cannot accommodate them, e.g. if they work only on Saturdays. Practical timing difficulties can leave these workers struggling to keep up with the latest developments without proper training. Organizations must give this their full attention to ensure their libraries continue to offer a quality service, and that they are fulfilling their obligations to their staff.

Library managers need to be aware of the specific training demands of flexible workers as the flexible workforce continues to increase in size and importance. Failure to develop these workers will pose serious implications for the skills profile of the library and information workforce. Managers can and must adapt their training practices and policies to maximise the benefits of employing flexible workers. This must include paying due attention to their working conditions and proper regard for their equality of opportunity.

Women's work

There is a danger that increasing economic pressure on library services will reinforce the stereotypical image of library assistants' jobs as 'women's work'. As libraries attempt to save on staff costs so the numbers of flexible posts increase. The ability to work the number of hours they wish, within certain guidelines and more or less when they wish, means that these posts are very attractive to women with domestic responsibilities. The employer is able to offer attractive packages for women with dependent children and, as explained above, can increase its labour supply significantly at the same time.

Although many organizations in both public and private sector are investigating the possibility of more flexible working practices to encourage women to return to work, and it could be argued that anything that assists women who want to enter or re-enter employment is a step forward, there is a real risk of 'ghettoising' library assistants. The more that library support staff work is seen as a nice and convenient job for a woman who can fit her hours of work around her domestic commitments, the fewer full-time career posts will be offered and the more the stereotype and occupational segregation will be reinforced. The more an occupation is dominated by women the less it pays, and the fewer opportunities for promotion and training exist. Occupational crowding in the library sector is still prevalent (Johnson, 1987). This causes salaries to be driven down and enables employers to continue paying lower salaries because the labour market will tolerate it.

The assumption that female library assistants are working for extrinsic financial reasons rather than for intrinsic satisfaction is outdated, unfair and, more importantly, untrue. As chapter 1 explained, library support staff are often positively drawn towards library employment, are very committed, and see it as more than simply a pleasant way to earn pin-money. However, it seems that many library organizations' pay and grading structures are based on such obsolete attitudes towards women. However, library employers,

> ...cannot claim to be eradicating inequality of opportunity if they sustain grading levels and structures which are based on outdated attitudes towards women and women's pay (NALGO, 1989, p. 8).

Women's skills and training have traditionally been systematically downgraded and undervalued (Beechey and Perkins, 1987). Equal pay legislation does not address this problem and the result, i.e. the divide that traditionally exists between men and women's work. The latter, whether at home or in the workplace, has always been regarded as less skilled and valuable than that of men. Library assistants and particularly paraprofessionals are now undertaking increasingly complex and responsible tasks, they have considerable knowledge of their organizations and the services they provide and yet they are generally only offered a limited career ladder.

Training potentially offers women the opportunity to redress some of the inequalities they suffer in employment (Equal Opportunities Commission, 1991) but unfortunately women also seem to be at a disadvantage here too. Most training employers offer is available to their (mainly male) full-time employees, while the (predominantly female) part-time employees are offered little training. Simply by mainly providing training for full-time workers, organizations are failing to offer training to huge numbers of women. It has also been suggested that different types of training are offered to different categories of worker: unskilled and semi-skilled employees tending to receive short induction and informal on-the-job training, if they received any training at all; clerical and secretarial workers tending to receive technical training; and managerial or higher administrative workers the only group being offered developmental training.

Moreover, although Labour Force Surveys (e.g. Labour Market Quarterly Report, 1995) show that women now receive slightly more job-related training than men, the nature of the training is not the same for both groups. The increase in training for women is linked to increased induction training for women returners, rather than a general increase in training for all women workers. Men are more likely to receive off-the-job training than women, while women are more likely to receive informal, on-the-job training. The former is more likely to result in qualifications which may then be used as transferable experience, increasing a worker's human capital and value in the labour market (McGiveney, 1994).

Library employers must recognise the need to attract and retain good female support staff by offering better training and development opportunities. Training plays a crucial role in workforce planning strategies as it is the main process by which the composition of the existing workforce can be changed. (Manpower Services Commission, 1981). Library managers must develop and adopt an equal opportunities policy which states a commitment to equality of opportunity (Morris, 1993) which can help break down the division between male and female jobs and the differences in wages, promotion possibilities and scope for development that result.

Conclusions

The efficient and effective use of human resources is vital in highly labour intensive organizations like libraries and information services. Recent rapid economic and social transition has focused attention on the need for the most profitable utilisation of staff to meet the objectives of the library or information service. Ideally, however, workforce strategies should not be developed reactively. Management should conduct periodic reviews of the library's organizational structure rather than waiting for a crisis to occur. They should try to be proactive not reactive as workforce planning strategies can help library service recognise and meet the emerging change in the workplace and workforce, and so manage these changes more effectively.

The pursuit of flexibility both as a way of improving the organization for the employer, and as a method of maximising employee productivity is a strategy library and information organizations are increasingly adopting to cope with uncertainty and change. However, for flexibility to work successfully it needs to be accompanied by management appreciation of the potential pitfalls as well as the manifold benefits to organizations. The support staff workforce has been transformed, and, to keep pace, management attitudes and strategies must adapt and change too. There is a need for managers to try to come to terms with the motivation and attitudes to work of flexible library support staff because of the obvious implication for managers for maintaining the effectiveness of the service and for promoting the job satisfaction and morale of this category of workers, especially as:

> ...part-time employment is here to stay and there is a need to increase our understanding of this work category (Fields and Thakur, 1991, p. 20).

Handling the potential conflict and problems that can arise from the introduction of more flexible working schedules is challenging for both senior and middle managers. The evidence suggests that libraries and information services have generally managed to successfully increase the numbers of flexible support staff workers employed in ways which now afford new opportunities for workers and the organizations which employ them. This has not happened suddenly nor without effort, however. It is clear that while flexible working offers benefits and drawbacks to both employer and employee, the employment of flexible workers is only appropriate and successful if there is full management commitment to fair employment policies - as demanded in law - and decent working conditions.

Notes

1. Goulding, A. (1993), *Managing Public Library Support Staff in Times of Change,* p. 295
2. Ibid, p. 117
3. Ibid, p. 180

7 Summary and conclusions

> Helping people believe in the importance of their work is essential, especially when other forms of certainty and security have disappeared (Kanter, 1989, p. 85).

The quotes from library staff in the preceding chapters demonstrate that library support staff do believe in the importance of what they do. They gain great satisfaction from serving the public, perceive their work as socially significant, and are aware of the value and meaning both of their jobs and of their work. However, other evidence proves that change can have a significant effect on this organizational commitment and satisfaction with work.

Support staff and the changing climate

The relationship between organizational commitment, job satisfaction and performance is complex but it would appear to be advantageous for employees to hold a strong belief in the organizational goals and values, a willingness to exert considerable effort on behalf of the organization, and a strong desire to remain part of that organization (Glisson and Durick, 1988). Commitment is likely to be higher when employees feel the organization is dependable and truly interested in their welfare. Commitment is more than passive loyalty to an organization. Rather, it is an active relationship in which individuals are willing to give something of themselves to an organization in return for certain rewards or outcomes (Steers, 1984). This constitutes a 'psychological contract' between employer and employee. When the exchange of values is felt to be fair, the employee can expect to feel good about work and have a positive relationship with the organization. When the exchange of values is felt to be unfair, the employee might develop bad attitudes, lose the desire to work hard, or even leave the organization (Schermerhorn et al, 1991).

Declining staffing levels and the commensurate rise in workload for those staffing libraries have left many in library services disheartened. Pressure to work harder can leave staff feeling 'put upon' and under considerable strain. Support staff often feel that changes are made with little thought to what the effects further down the chain of command might be. These pressures can leave support staff feeling very depressed about their own positions and that of their library service:

> I'm very, very frustrated now, and disillusioned with what's happening at the moment, and cynical. Those are the words that spring to mind (paraprofessional, metropolitan borough).[1]

Library services need the full commitment of all staff if they are to meet and make the most of the challenges facing them. The attitudes of the support staff, making up the majority of library workers, are therefore crucial. Unfortunately, support staff often feel confused, anxious, and overburdened by their duties and the rate of change occurring in their services. Two crucial factors in their disenchantment are a perceived lack of communication from senior management, and a feeling that they are not being rewarded or appreciated for the extra effort they are expending. Loyalty is a two-way street and the level of commitment employees display will depend upon the commitment the organization shows them. Support staff need a demonstration that management is truly concerned with their welfare.

Management response

Management must be sure to communicate appreciation for work beyond the call of duty, especially over a long sustained period, and recognise the important role that such communications play in the maintenance of organizational commitment and morale.

Job redesign

One strategy that managers could use to strengthen commitment and demonstrate their confidence in their support staff is the adoption of work design principles which can encourage job commitment and involvement and satisfy the need for creative work, independent judgement and personal discretion (Thapisa, 1990). Although the theories and methods of work design were generally constructed in times of expansion, there is evidence

135

that they may help maintain morale and satisfaction in difficult times too as new challenges and experiences are encountered. Research has found that although work redesign will not necessarily improve workers' performance, employees do perceive that changes have been made to their jobs and express higher levels of motivation, satisfaction or both as a result (Griffin, 1991).

In fact, changes to assistants' jobs have been quite substantial and the broadening of their role, responsibilities and skills has often brought about a change in management attitude towards this category of staff, and in staff attitudes towards their work. Staff without professional library qualifications have gradually taken over much of the day-to-day running of libraries and service points, and this has led to a greater willingness by management to recognise their skills and value. As layers of management have been removed, so support staff have come to play an increasingly important role, and so they are recognised as being very valuable for the achievement of the organizational goals:

> I think the fact that [support staff] are out there running branches and working under a great deal of pressure, I think they probably get more respect and are valued more highly than they were in the past (librarian, London borough).[2]

However, although senior managers often stress their awareness of the changes that have taken place with regard to support staff roles and responsibilities, and emphasise how much they value their assistants, this message does not always reach staff on the ground. Staff may also feel that lip service is not enough anymore. They want action that proves in hard terms just how much management values them.

The working environment

Support staff know that much of what they do is not clerical or secretarial although they are often still paid on a clerical scale. Increasingly, assistants believe they deserve a promotion line of support staff grades that increase in difficulty of assignment, personal contacts and degree of responsibility. The nature of support staff work has changed rapidly and quite dramatically and the onus is now on managers to acknowledge the value of their support staff by providing career structures that reflect their value and worth to the organization. Support staff are generally eager and willing to take on more responsibility and excited at the prospect of enlarged, more influential positions. The challenge for library managers is to acknowledge and respect the new status of this category of staff and credit them for their more sophisticated level of work.

Although there have been senior library assistants in libraries for years, the introduction suggested that a 'new' type of library support staff has emerged as a result of changing environmental and organizational circumstances. The emergence of the paraprofessional is vivid evidence of this. These higher level assistants are often now involved in quite demanding work. Nevertheless, the job title 'library assistant' is still used to describe various levels of support staff ranging from volunteers to the professional with a library qualification. Local variations, needs and preferences continue to take precedence over the establishment of nation-wide standards and classification. There now needs to be formal recognition of the different types of support staff and demarcations within the support staff structure. Until support staff relationships with regard to one another, and other library personnel, are clarified, there will continue to be confusion over what their role is. Giving this higher grade of support staff a clearly defined sense of identity in their library services will confer on them a special status and will also address the confusion that still exists between professional and paraprofessional duties.

Without this recognition and structural change support staff will feel increasingly disenchanted with their lack of career prospects:

> However hard you work and however much responsibility you
> get, it just doesn't matter. I don't really feel a sense of loyalty.
> There's nothing really to work for (library assistant, London
> borough).[3]

The accumulation of these pressures and strains on support staff may eventually have the effect of making some staff leave and encouraging others to switch off mentally and fail to exert their best possible effort. People often put loyalty to their career above loyalty to the organization but by offering careers, not just jobs, libraries can nurture a pool of talent. If a service is to retain its best staff, there must be a commitment to career development and training.

The Fielden Report (John Fielden Consultancy, 1993) concluded that the wider range of tasks that support staff in the future will be expected to perform will have far-reaching implications for the scale and coverage of training. Moreover, the recruitment criteria of support staff posts will need to take into account the ability of the individual to grow in terms of skills and competence. It is, thus, management's responsibility to ensure that the potential of all support staff is fully realised and developed. Too often, however, the amount and effectiveness of training received by library support staff is reliant upon the motivation of the line manager and on the presence of a dynamic, committed individual co-ordinating training efforts.

The key to success for libraries is how well they use and involve their support staff. A different management style is needed which recognises the need to develop assistants' skills so that management can place greater trust in them. Effective management-employee communication is a pre-requisite for employee loyalty, commitment and motivation and thus a successful library service.

There is evidence that library managers are becoming more open, participative and consultative. Support staff now often have the impression that they are working in a far more relaxed environment and that the team approach is very much the rule. There is increasing integration and discussion between different levels of staff, whether just in the day-to-day running of the service, in training sessions, or in meetings. Although a decline in loyalty and motivation can be a problem for organizations undergoing change, participative techniques can help increase commitment and job satisfaction. In libraries, the devolvement of many supervisory responsibilities to branch and paraprofessional level can add new interest to jobs and encourage enthusiasm for the service's mission and development.

Good library managers acknowledge the social responsibility of their organizations for their staff and accept that it is their duty to involve and consult staff. Library support staff are growing more demanding in this respect too. Research shows that employees are increasingly better informed, relatively better educated, and more complex than every before, and they demand a more responsive and flexible working environment (Zeffrane and Mayo, 1994). Managers therefore need to ensure that staff are kept fully informed about the organization's current circumstances and future plans.

Management thus has to keep pace with the changes that have been taking place within the support staff workforce of libraries. Fewer employees now accept management decisions without question, and demand consultation and more say in shaping their working conditions and environment. For example, the traditional barrier that existed between 'professional' and 'non-professional' work in libraries is being increasingly challenged with many support staff believing they deserve recognition in their own right and viewing the bar that prevents their promotion to higher supervisory grades as outdated and unfair. It has been suggested that,

> ...today's employees tend to bring more abilities, higher expectations, and a greater desire for self-responsibility to their workplace than did their predecessors (Loher and Noe, 1985, p. 352).

138

Because of this, staff expect a say in the decisions that affect their jobs, and are better able to articulate their demands. Nowadays, there is a greater tendency to look for personal growth and development through work. Support staff in library services can be helped in this by far-sighted managers who understand their motivations and working needs in the face of the enormous changes taking place in the library workplace and in the wider environment.

This book does not presume to claim to have all the answers. Rather, its aim is to stimulate debate and open discussion about the issues involved in managing change for support staff, a hitherto rather neglected but vital section of the library workforce. An analysis of the current library environment highlights the significance of support staff to the continuing development of library services. However, the attitudes of this group of workers towards their work and their views of library services are quite distinct from those of professional librarians and raise important questions about their management. The importance of keeping all staff fully informed of developments cannot be overemphasised:

> ...inform us and we become a stronger team to cope with change and restructure (Public Library Journal, 1992, p. 124).

Notes

1. Goulding, A. (1993), *Managing Public Library Support Staff in Times of Change,* p. 481
2. Ibid, p. 463
3. Ibid, p. 484

Bibliography

Appelbaum, S. H. (1991), 'How to slim successfully and ethically; two case studies of "downsizing"', *Leadership and Organization Development Journal,* 12(3), pp. 11-16.

Appelbaum, S. H. and Finestone, D., 'Revisiting career plateauing', *Managerial Psychology*, 9(5), pp. 12-21.

Asheim, L. (1967), 'Manpower. A call to action', *Library Journal*, 92(9), pp. 1795-1797.

Aslib (1995), *Review of the Public Library Service in England and Wales* Aslib, London.

Assistant Librarian (1991), 'Interchange' *Assistant Librarian*, 84(8), pp. 114.

Aukland, M. (1990), 'Surviving the skills shortage: is there a problem?', *Information and Library Manager,* 9(2), 4-7.

Bach, S. (1994), 'The working environment', in Sisson, K. (ed.), *Personnel Management*, Blackwell Business, Oxford, pp. 117-149

Baker, D. (1986), *What about the Workers? A study of non-professional staff in library work*, AAL, London.

Bardwick, J. M. (1988), *The Plateauing Trap*, Bantam Books, Toronto.

Beechey, V. and Perkins, T. (1989), *A Matter of Hours,* Polity, Oxford.

Billings, C. D. and Kern, B. (1990), 'Sources of satisfaction and dissatisfaction among library paraprofessionals', *LLA Bulletin*, 52(4), pp. 171-178.

Blanchard, K. (1995), 'Shower people with information', *Executive Excellence,* 12(4), pp. 11-12.

Blyton, P. (1994), *'Working Hours',* in Sisson, K. (ed.), *Personnel Management*, Blackwell Business, Oxford, pp. 495-526.

Bold, R. (1982), 'Librarian burnout' *Library Journal*, Vol. 107, pp. 2048-2051.

Buch, K. and Aldridge, J. (1990), 'Downsizing challenges and OD interventions: a matching strategy', *Journal of Managerial Psychology*, 5(4), pp. 32-37.

Buchanan, D. A. (1994), 'Principles and practice in work design', in Sisson, K. (ed.), *Personnel Management*, Blackwell Business, Oxford, pp. 85-116.

Buchanan, D. A. and Huczynski, A. A. (1985), *Organizational Behaviour,* Prentice Hall, London.

Bunge, C. A. (1989), 'Stress in the library workplace', *Library Trends,* 38(1), pp. 92-102.

Butler, W. F. (1986), *An Investigation into Levels of Job Satisfaction Among Non-professional Staff at Keele University Library*, Major Project for MA Library Studies, Manchester Polytechnic Department of Library and Information Studies, Manchester.

Bywaters, D. R. (1988), 'Managing during downsizing', *Executive Excellence*, 5(7), pp. 13-14.

Cameron, K. S. (1994), 'Strategies for successful organizational downsizing', *Human Resource Management*, 33(2), pp. 189-211.

Carnazza, J. P., Korman, A. K., Ference, T. P. and Stoner, J. A. F. (1981) 'Plateaued and non-plateaued managers: factors in job performance', *Journal of Management*, 7(2), pp. 7-25.

Corrall, S. (1995), 'Strategy; who needs it?', *Library Manager*, Volume 3, January, p. 9.

Castelyn, M. (1991), 'Affiliated membership - land of cream and honey', *Personnel Training and Education*, 8(2), pp. 38-43.

Cevallos, E. E. and Kratz, C. E. (1990), 'Training for public library services', *Journal of Library Administration*, 12(2), pp. 27-45.

Chwe, S. S. (1978), 'A comparative study of job satisfaction: cataloguers and reference librarians in University Libraries', *Journal of Academic Librarianship*, 4(3), pp. 139-143.

Clemens, B. (1983), *Career Ladders for Support Staff in University Libraries*, PhD, Florida.

Clemons, J. G. (1994), 'A communication office in the year 2010', *Communications World*, 11(1), pp. 42-43.

Coleman, P. (1990) Comment Library Review, 39(5): 5,6

Conroy, B. (1978) *Library Staff Development and Continuing Education*, Libraries Unlimited, Littleton, Colorado.

Core, J. K. (1991), 'Non-professional training and development: organizational purpose and individual satisfaction in the small college library', Personnel Training and Education, 8(1), pp. 14-27.

Cowan B. M. and Usherwood, B. (1992), 'Automation routes past and present: the training implications', *Journal of Librarianship and Information Science*, 24(3), pp. 139-148.

Cropley, J. (1992), 'Budgeting in Special Libraries', *Serials*, 5(1), pp. 58-61.

Dakers, H. (1995), 'The Impact of S/NVQs', *Library Association Record,*. 97(11), p. 34.

Daum, P. B. (1987), 'Recession a challenge for special librarians', *Canadian Library Journal,* 44(5), pp. 299-302.

Davis, A., Cox, T., and Beale, D. (1991), 'Exposure to repetitive computer-based work', *Personnel Review*, 20(1), pp. 3-12.

Doe, P., (1994), 'Creating a resilient organization', *Canadian Business Review,* 21(2), pp. 22-25.

Equal Opportunities Commission (1991), *Women and Training: a review*, EOC, Manchester.

Estabrook, L., Bird, C., and Gilmore, F. L. (1990), 'Job satisfaction: does automation make a difference?', *Journal of Library Administration*, 13(1/2), pp. 175-194.

Evans, D. (1992), *Supervisory Management,* Cassel Educational Limited, London, third edition.

Fields, M. W. and Thacker, J. W. (1991), 'Job-related attitudes of part-time and full-time workers', *Journal of Management Psychology*, 6(2), pp. 17-20.

Financing our Public Library Service: four subjects for debate. A consultative paper , 1988, HMSO, London.

Fitch, D. K. (1990), 'Job satisfaction among library support staff in Alabama Academic Libraries', *College and Research Libraries*, 51(4), pp. 313-320.

Flynn, N. (1990), *Public Sector Management*, Harvester Wheatsheaf, Hemel Hempstead.

Gattiker, U. E. and Howg, L (1990), 'Information technology and quality of work life: comparing users with non-users', *Journal of Business and Psychology,* 5(2), pp. 237-260.

Gill, S. (1981), 'New direction for library paraprofessionals', *Wilson Library Bulletin,* 55(5), pp. 368-369, 397.

Glisson, C. and Durick, M. (1988), 'Predictors of job satisfaction and organizational commitment in human service organizations', *Administrative Science Quarterly*, 33(1), pp. 61-81.

Glogoff, S. J. and Flynn, J. P. (1990), 'End analysis: aligning library planning resources and commitment to ILS staff training', *Journal of Library Administration,* 12(2), pp. 13-26.

Goulding, A. (1993), *Managing Public Library Support Staff in Times of Change,* PhD thesis, Department of Information Studies, University of Sheffield.

Goulding, A. and Kerslake, E. (1995), 'A firm commitment to a flexible future', *Library Association Record,* 97(11), pp. 605-607.

Govan, J. F. (1988), 'The creeping invisible hand: entrepreneurial librarianship', *Library Journal,* 113(1), pp. 35-38.

Greenhalgh, L. (1982), 'Managing the job insecurity crisis', *Human Resource Management,* 22(4), pp. 431-444.

Griffin, R. W. (1991), 'Effects of work redesign on employee perceptions, attitudes and behaviours: a long-term investigation', *Academy of Management Journal,* 34(2), pp. 425-435.

Gruneberg, M. M. (1979), *Understanding Job Satisfaction,* Macmillan, London.

Hackman, J. R. and Lawler, E. E. (1971), 'Employee reactions to job characteristics', *Journal of Applied Psychology,* 53(3), pp. 259-286.

Hackman, J. R. and Oldham, G. R. (1976), *Work Redesign,* Addison Wesley, Reading, Mass.

Hales, C. (1993), *Managing Through Organization: the management process, forms of organization and the work of managers,* Routledge, London.

Hall, J. (1982), 'No growth and low mobility in libraries: an overview of origins, consequences and solutions', in Hall, J. (ed.), *Fighting Professional Stagnation. Staff development in a period of low mobility. Papers presented at a short course 6-7 April 1982* Leeds Polytechnic School of Librarianship, Leeds, pp. 3-16.

Hall, D. T. and Gordon, F. E. (1973), 'Effects of career choices on married women', *Journal of Applied Psychology,* 38(1), pp. 42-48.

Hannabuss, S. (1983), 'Motivational theories and managerial questions', *Information and Library Manager,* 2(4), pp. 98-111.

Hannon, M. (1982), 'Professional stagnation in the University Library: management problems and opportunities', in Hall, J. (ed.), *Fighting Professional Stagnation. Staff development in a period of low mobility. Papers presented at a short course 6-7 April 1982* Leeds Polytechnic School of Librarianship, Leeds, pp. 74-80.

Hardy, C. (1987), 'Effective retrenchment: human resource implications', *Journal of General Management*, 12(3), pp. 76-92.

Harrison, B. (1993), 'The dark side of flexible production', *National Productivity Review,* 13(4), pp. 479-501.

Harvey, J. F. and Spyers-Duran, P. (1984), *Austerity Management in Library Organizations*, Scarecrow, Metuchen.

Hayes, P., Glastonbury, B., Marks, E., Stein, M., and Frost, N. (1989), *Social Work in Crisis: a study of conditions in six local authorities*, NALGO, London.

Henty, M. (1989), 'Performance indicators in higher education libraries', *British Journal of Academic Librarianship*, 4(3), pp. 177-191.

Herzberg, F. Mausner, B. and Snyderman, B. (1959), *The Motivation to Work*, Wiley, New York.

Hodges, J. E. (1990), 'Stress in the library', *Library Association Record*, 92(10), pp. 751-754.

Hofstetter, A. (1982), 'The role of the library technician', *Bulletin of the Quebec Library Association*, 23(1), pp. 26-33.

House, D. and Moon, C. (1994), 'The new academic librarian', in Harris, C. (ed.), *The New University Library: issues for the '90s and beyond. Essays in honour of Ian Rogerson,* Taylor Graham, London, pp. 73-88.

Huws, U., Hurstfield, J. and Holtmaat, R. (1989), *What Price Flexibility? The casualisation of women's employment*, Low Pay Unit, London.

Igbafe, D. O. E. (1984), 'The place of library assistants in promoting the image of an academic library: a personal view', *Bendel Library Journal*, 7(1), pp. 59-65.

Ilgen, D. R., Taylor, C. D. and Taylor, M. S. (1979), 'Consequences of individual feedback on behaviour in organizations', *Journal of Applied Psychology*, 64(4), pp. 349-371.

Imberman, W. (1989), 'Managers and downsizing', *Business Horizons*, Sept/Oct, pp. 28-33.

Isacco, J. M. (1985), 'Work spaces, satisfaction and productivity in libraries', *Library Journal*, 110(8), pp. 27-30.

Jacobs, D. (1988), 'Maintaining morale during and after downsizing', *Management Solutions*, 33(4), pp. 5-13.

Jick, T. D. (1985), 'As the ax falls: budget cuts and the experience of stress in organizations', in Beehr, T. A. and Baghat, R. S. (eds.), *Human Stress and Cognition in Organizations,* Wiley, New York, pp. 83-114

Jick, T. D. and Murray, V. V. (1982), 'The management of hard times: budget cutbacks in public sector organizations', *Organization Studies*, 3(2), pp. 141-169.

Joint Funding Councils' Libraries Review Group (1993), *Report,* Bristol, HEFCE

John Fielden Consultancy (1993), *Supporting Expansion: a report on human resource management in academic libraries, for the Joint Funding Councils' Libraries Review Group* Bristol, HEFCE.

Johnson, N. P. (1987), 'Comparable worth in libraries: a legal analysis', *Law Library Journal,* Vol. 79, summer, pp. 367-386.

Jones, K. (1984), *Conflict and Change in Library Organizations: people, power and services,* London, Bingley.

Jones, N. and Jordan, P. (1987), *Staff Management in Library and Information Work*, Gower, Aldershot: second edition.

Jowell, R., Brook, L. and Taylor, B. (eds.) with Prior, G. (1991), *British Social Attitudes: the 8th report*, Dartmouth Publishing Company, Dartmouth.

Katzell, R. A. and Thompson, D. E. (1990), 'Work motivation: theory and practice', *American Psychologist*, 45(2), pp. 144-153.

Kelly, R. (1990), 'Library sweatshop: a view from the bottom', *Los Angeles Book Review,* May 20, p. 15.

King, P. (1989), *Privatisation and Public Libraries*, EMBLA, East Midlands.

Kinlaw, D. C. (1995), *The Practice of Empowerment*, Gower, Aldershot.

Kirkland, J. J. (1991), 'Equity and entitlement: internal barriers to improving the pay of academic librarians', *College and Research Libraries*, 52(4), pp. 375-380.

Kiss, S. (1994), 'Uniting the downsized firm', *Computing Canada*, 20(9), p. 3.

Klingner, D. C. (1979), 'Job descriptions: new uses for a familiar tool', *Law Library Journal,* 72(1), pp. 65-67.

Klitzman, S. and Stellman, J. M. (1989), 'The impact of the physical environment on the psychological well-being of office workers', *Social Science and Medicine*, 29(6), pp. 733-742.

KPMG Peat Marwick (1994), *DNH Study: contracting out in public libraries,* KPMG Peat Marwick, London.

Labour Market Quarterly Report (1995), 'November, 1995', Department for Education and Employment, Sheffield.

Lambert, C. (1985), *Expenditure Cuts in Public Libraries and their Effects on Services,* The Library Campaign, Sheffield.

Larson, T. (1981), 'The case for using paraprofessionals', *ERIC Teaching Guide: ED205207.*

Lawler, E. E. (1971), *Pay and Organizational Effectiveness: a psychological view*, McGraw Hill, New York.

Lee, R. (1994) 'Recruitment in context', *Librarian Career Development*, 2(2), pp. 3-7.

Levett, J. (1981), 'Paraprofessional workers in four fields: a comparative study', *Australian Library Journal*, 30(2), pp. 47-54.

Levine, C. H. (1978), 'Organizational decline and cutback management', *Public Administration Review*, 38(2), pp. 316-325.

Levine, C. H. (1979), 'More on cutback management. Hard questions for hard times', *Public Administration Review*, 39(1), pp. 179-182.

Levine, C. H. (1984), 'Retrenchment, human resource erosion and the role of the personnel manager', *Public Personnel Management Journal*, Fall, pp. 249-263.

Library Work (1989), 'The case for regrading', *Library Work*, 5 July, pp. 4-7.

Line, M. and Robertson, K (1989), 'Staff development in libraries', *British Journal of Academic Librarianship*, 4(3), pp. 161-175.

Linquist, P. A. (1990), 'Managing on the edge', *Best's Review (prop/casualty)*, 90(11), pp. 34-36, 84.

Lippet, G. and Lippet, R. (1984), 'Human downsizing: organizational renewal versus organizational depression', *SAM Advanced Management Journal*, Summer, pp. 15-21.

Loher, B. T. and Noe, R. A. (1985), 'A meta-analysis of the relation of job characteristics to job satisfaction', *Journal of Applied Psychology*, 70(2), pp. 280-289.

Luce, S. R. (1983), 'Human Resource policy under pressure: learning from restraint', *Canadian Business Review*, 10(1), pp. 24-27.

Lund, K. and Patterson, H. (1994) *Customer Care,* Library Association, London.

Maehr, M. L. (1989), 'Building job commitment among employees', *Library Trends,* 38(1), pp. 3-10.

Manpower Services Commission, (1981), *No Barriers Here,* MSC, Sheffield.

Martyn, J. (1991), 'Factors affecting the future of libraries', *ASLIB Proceedings,* 43(9), pp. 277-285.

Maslow, A. H. (1943), 'A theory of human motivation', *Psychological Review*, Vol. 50, pp. 370-396.

McCann, J. C., Davis, S. E., Trainer, D. J. and Waller, D. K. (1990), 'Restructuring support staff classification levels for academic health sciences library positions', *Bulletin of the Medical Library Association,* 78(3), pp. 293-301.

McGivney, V. (1994), Wasted Potential: training and career progression for part-time and temporary workers, NIACE, Leicester.

McGoon, C., (1994), 'What role shall we play today?', *Communication World,* 11(7), 1994, pp. 12-16.

McGrath, H. (1995), *A survey of violence in libraries*, MA Dissertation, Loughborough University of Technology, Loughborough.

McKee, B. (1987), *Public Libraries - into the 1990's?*, AAL, Newcastle Under Lyme.

McKee, B (1989), *Planning Library Services* Clive Bingley, London.

McNally, P. F. (1982), 'Job motivation and satisfaction of reference staff in public libraries', *Argus*, 11(1), pp. 9-15.

Mehrabian, A. (1990), 'Effects of affective and informational characteristics of work environments on worker satisfaction', *Imagination, Cognition and Personality,* 9(4), pp. 293-301.

Miller, K. I., Ellis, B. H., Zook, E. G., Lyles, J. S. (1990), 'An integrated model of communication, stress and burnout in the workplace', *Communication Research*, 17(3), pp. 300-326.

Moore, R. (1979), 'Team librarianship', *Assistant Librarian*, 72(12), pp. 154-157.

Moran, R. F. (1980), 'Improving the organizational design of academic libraries Journal of Academic Librarianship, 6(3), pp. 140-145.

Morris, B. (1990), 'Surviving the skills shortage: exploring the options, *Information and Library Manager,* 9(2), 11-22.

Morris, B. (1993), *Training for Women*, LAPL, London.

Muller, R. H. (1965), 'Principles governing the employment of nonprofessional personnel in University Libraries', *College and Research Libraries,* 26(May), pp. 225-226.

NALGO (1989), *Library Staff: guidelines for action* NALGO, London.

Nauratil, M. J. (1989), *The Alienated Librarian*, Greenwood Press, New York.

Naylor, K. (1994), 'Part-time working in Great Britain - an historical analysis', *Employment Gazette,* December, pp. 473-484.

Nettleford, B. A. (1985), *Paraprofessionalism in Irish Libraries: the potential for development of a library technician grade*, FLAI Thesis; Irish Library Association, Dun Laoghaire.

Nettleford, B. A. (1989), 'Paraprofessionalism in Librarianship', *International Library Review*, 21(4), pp. 519-531.

Oberg, L. R. (1992), 'The emergence of the paraprofessional in academic libraries: perceptions and realities', *College and Research Libraries*, 53(2), pp. 99-112.

Oberg, L. R., Mentges, M. E., McDermott, P. N. and Harusadangkul, V. (1992), 'The role, status and working conditions of paraprofessionals: a national survey of academic libraries', *College and Research Libraries*, 53(3), pp. 215-238.

O'Connor, E. J., Peters, L. H., Pooyan, A., Weekley, J., Frank, B. and Erenkrantz, B. (1984), 'Situational constraints: effects on performance, affective reactions and turnover: a field replication and extension', *Journal of Applied Psychology,* 69(4), pp. 663-672.

Odini, C. (1990), 'The management of change in a library service', *Library Review,* 39(4), pp. 8-20.

Oulton, T. (1991), *Strategies in Action: public library management and public expenditure constraints*, Library Association, London.

Pankhurst, R. (1984), 'The effects of professional stagnation on the organization', *Australasian College Libraries*, 2(1), pp. 13-18.

Personnel Management & Lloyds Masters Consulting, (1994), *Training Survey Results 1994,* Lloyds Masters Consulting, Twickenham.

Prasad, H. N. and Singh, S. N. (1989), 'A study into the effect of job anxiety on the job satisfaction of professional librarian staff: a case study', *Lucknow Librarian*, 21(4), pp. 159-181.

Public Library Journal (1992), 'Changing services: review and restructure: the Public Libraries Weekend School', *Public Library Journal,* 7(5), pp. 123-125.

Raddon, R, (ed.) (1991), *People and Work. Human and industrial relations in library and information work*, Bingley, London.

Rolfe, H. with Taylor, P., Casey, B., Christie, I., & McRae, S., *Employers' Role in the Supply of Intermediate Skills*, Employment Department, Sheffield.

Rubin, I. S. (1984), 'Marasmus or recovery? The effect of cutbacks in federal agencies', *Social Sciences Quarterly*, 65, pp. 74-88.

Russel, J. C. (1989), 'Cutbacks, management and human relations: meanings for organizational theory and research', *Human Relations*, 42(8), pp. 671-689.

Russell, N. J. (1985), 'Professional and non-professional in libraries: the need for a new relationship', *Journal of Librarianship*, 17(4), pp. 293-310.

Russell, N. J. (1986), *The Job Satisfaction of Non-professional Library Staff*, Leeds Polytechnic Department of Library and Information   Studies, Research Report No 20.

Sahl, R. J. (1994), 'Defined job contributions', *Human Resource Professional,* 7(1), pp. 3-6.

Scarrott, M. (1989), 'Non-professional staff: an overview', *Library Work*, 4, pp. 16-19.

Schermerhorn, J. R., Hunt, J. G. and Osborn, R. N. (1991), *Managing Organizational Behaviour*, John Wiley & Sons, New York: fourth edition.

Schneider, M. S. (1991), 'Stress and job satisfaction among employees in a public library system with a focus on public service', *Library and Information Science Research,* 13(4), pp. 385-404.

Shields, M. (1988), 'The great divide', *Library Work*, 1, pp. 21-23.

Smith, F. W. (1990), 'Our human side of quality', *Quality Progress*, Oct, pp. 19-21.

Steel, B. S. and Lovrich, N. P. (1987), 'Comparable worth: the problematic politicization of a public personnel issue', *Public Personnel Management,* Vol. 16, spring, pp. 23-36.

Steers, R. M. (1984), *Introduction to Organizational Behaviour*, Scott, Foreman & Co., Glenview; Illinois: second edition.

Stott, K. and Walker, A. (1995), *Teams, teamwork and teambuilding* Prentice Hall, New York.

Sub-committee on In-service Training (1962), 'In-service training. The report of the sub-committee on in-service training', *Library Association Record*, Vol. 29, May, pp. 171-175.

Sumsion, J., Creaser, C., and Hanratty, C. (1995), *LISU Annual Statistics,* Library and Information Statistics Unit, Loughborough.

Taylor, G. S. (1994), 'Realistic job previews in the trucking industry', *Journal of Management Issues*, 6(4), pp. 457-473.

Taylor, J. (1981), 'The lowest of the low: library assistants in public libraries', *Librarians for Social Change*, 9(1), pp 14-15.

Thapisa, A. P. N. (1989), 'The burden of mundane tasks: library assistants' perceptions of work', *British Journal of Academic Librarianship*, 4(3), pp. 137-160.

Thapisa, A. P. N. (1989a), *The Meaningfulness of Work: improving the quality of work life through job enrichment* PhD, University of Sheffield, Sheffield.

Thapisa, A. P. N. (1990), 'The triple tier organizational structure: improving the quality of work life through job redesign', *British Journal of Academic Librarianship*, 5(2), pp. 95-117.

Toolis, L. (1976), 'Invisible people: library assistants', *Emergency Librarian*, 4(1), pp. 19-21.

Tombaugh, J. R. and White, L. P. (1990), 'Downsizing: an empirical assessment of survivors' perceptions in a post-layoff environment' *Organization Development Journal*, 8(2), pp. 32-43.

Ungarelli, D. L. and McNierney, M. (1983), 'A fee based model: administrative considerations in an academic library', *Drexel Library Quarterly*, 19(4), pp. 4-12.

Usherwood, B. (1989), *The Public Library as Public Knowledge*, Library Association, London.

Vaughn, W. J. and Dunn, J. D. (1974), 'A study of job satisfaction in six university libraries', *College and Research Libraries*, 35(3), pp. 161-177.

Veaner, A. B. (1982), 'Continuity or discontinuity - a persistent personnel issue in academic librarianship', *Advances in Library Administration and Organization,* Vol. 1, pp. 1-20.

Vincent, I. (1978), 'Womanpower! Part-time work and job sharing in libraries', *Australian Library Journal*, 27(20), pp. 330-333.

Wahba, S. P. (1978), 'Motivation, performance and job satisfaction of librarians', *Law Library Journal*, 7(2), pp. 270-278.

Wallace, V. (1992), *Who Manages the Library? The role of the paraprofessional*, Branch and Mobile Libraries Group of the Library Association, London.

Walby, S. (1990), *Theorizing Patriarchy,* Blackwell, Oxford.

Wallis, M. (1990), 'Surviving the skills shortage: an employer's view', *Information and Library Manager,* 9(2), pp. 8-10.

Waterman, R. H., Waterman, J. A., Collard, B. A. (1994), 'Toward a career-resilient workforce', *Harvard Business Review,* 72(4), pp. 87-95.

Webb, J. (1990), 'The non-professional in the academic library: education for paraprofessionalism', *Personnel Training and Education,* 7(2), pp. 21-30.

White, H. S. (1982), 'The management of change and the management of retrenchment', *Information and Library Manager,* 2(2), pp. 32, 47.

Winkworth, I. (1994), 'Libraries: adding value', *Bookseller,* 4505, 24 April, pp. 1207-1208.

Zeffrane, R. and Mayo, G. (1994), 'Rightsizing: socio economic sensibility and a visionary approach to workforce planning and employment relations in the nineties', *International Journal of Sociology and Social Policy,* 14(3/4/5), pp. 1-37.

Index

effect on environment 67, 92
effect on work patterns 125
training for 105
job description 65
job profile *see* job description
job sharing 124, 128
   see also flexible working, part-
   time working

Labour Force Surveys 132
library assistants
   career structure 23, 35, 78,
   129, 136
   contact with co-workers 38,
   83, 85, 102
   contact with users 18, 22, 32,
   42, 47, 83, 89, 99
   definition 19, 52, 55
   motivation of 26, 48, 54, 55,
   57, 74, 77, 79, 80, 101, 109
   role 9, 13, 34, 40, 52, 54, 57,
   86, 102, 136
   supervision 30, 70, 75, 77, 86,
   100, 101, 103, 137
   training 41, 50, 75, 89, 104,
   124, 131, 137
Library Association, The 14, 72,
   107
library budgets *see* budgets
Library Charter, The 90
Library and Information
   Commission 2
local government reorganization
   4, 70, 125

Maslow, Abraham 68
media *see* information media
mentoring 79

NVQs *see* S/NVQs

National Heritage, Department of
   see Department of National
   Heritage
National Vocational Qualifications
   see S/NVQs

one person libraries 42
organizational change
   communication 25, 39, 70, 88,
   95, 97, 117, 122
   effect on jobs 65, 85, 105,
   120, 122
   effect on management
   structures 102, 122, 137
   effect on organizational culture
   42, 112
   effect on services 120
   effect on staff 24, 39, 55, 84,
   87, 95, 105, 112, 134
   organizational decline as 7
organizational culture
   effect of change on 42, 112
   in libraries 138

paraprofessionals
   career structure 21, 35, 70, 74,
   78, 129, 136
   contact with co-workers 38,
   83, 85, 102
   contact with users 18, 32, 42,
   47, 83, 89, 99
   definition 14
   duties 19, 27, 53
   motivation 26, 48, 54, 56, 57,
   77, 79, 80, 109
   role 9, 17, 27, 34, 40, 52, 54,
   57, 96, 102, 111, 121, 136
   supervision 30, 70, 75, 77, 86,
   100, 103, 137
   training 41, 50, 76, 89, 104,
   124, 131, 137
parity *see* equality